J. J. Brown and Thomas E. Watson

J. J. Brown
and Thomas

E. Watson

*Georgia Politics
1912–1928*

BY

WALTER J. BROWN

ISBN 0-86554-322-4

J. J. Brown and Thomas E. Watson
Georgia Politics 1912–1928
Copyright © 1988
Walter J. Brown
Printed in the United States of America

The paper used in this publication meets
the minimum requirements of American National Standard
for Information Sciences—Permanence of Paper
for Printed Library Materials, ANSI Z39.48-1984

Library of Congress Cataloging-in-Publication Data
Walter J. Brown
J. J. Brown and Thomas E. Watson:
Georgia Politics, 1912–1928
by Walter J. Brown
156 p.   15 x 23 cm.
ISBN 0-86554-322-4 (alk. paper)

1. Brown, John Judson, 1865–1953.   2. Watson, Thomas
E. (Thomas Edward), 1856–1922.   3. Politicians—Georgia—Biography.   5.Georgia—Politics and government—
1865–1950.   6. Brown, Walter J.   I. Title.
F291.B72B76   1988
975.8'042'0922—dc19
[B]   88-13447
                                                                CIP

Contents

• CHAPTER I •

Political Baptism for a Boy of Nine

"You can go back to bed, Walter, they have stole your Pa's nomination."

These words were my initiation into the game of politics. The year was 1912, I was nine years old, and we were living in Toccoa at the North Georgia home of my banker brother-in-law. My mother had moved up from our home in nearby Bowman to take care of my sister and her first baby.

I had waited up most of the night to hear the news of my father's fate in the balloting for Commissioner of Agriculture at the state Democratic convention in Macon. In those days there was, of course, no radio and communication was generally poor. However, my brothers, Polk and Ves, were in Macon, and after the convention vote they left on the long automobile trip back to Toccoa. In the early morning hours of August 29 they brought the sad story to our temporary household.

Despite papa's clear plurality in the popular and county unit[1] votes in the August 1 primary, there had been much speculation around our house that a movement was afoot to prevent my father's nomination. In the primary papa had led in sixty counties and had a county unit vote of 142, incumbent James D. Price of Oconee County was second with 122 votes, and A. O. Blalock of Fayette County was third with 100. Although my father had a strong and loyal following among the farmers of Georgia, he realized he would have to get some support from the Blalock delegates if he hoped to secure a majority of the county unit votes.

On the first ballot, papa and Price were tied with 177 votes; Blalock received only two votes. William J. Harris, chairman of the convention and later a United States senator, immediately ordered a second ballot. Bedlam broke loose in the hall as delegates began running helter-skelter up and down the aisles, doing everything possible to prevent a stampede from their particular candidate. Papa was still aching from an accident in which he had almost been killed when thrown from his Maxwell Special car near Buckhead, outside Atlanta, on August 15, just two weeks prior to the convention. But he hurried from delegation to delegation contending that he was entitled to the nomination since he had led in the popular vote.

At this point Blalock formally withdrew from the contest. He then urged the convention not to nominate a can-

---

[1]Under the county unit system, long practiced by the Georgia Democratic Party and later enacted into law by the Neil White Primary Act of 1917, rural counties were given a decisive advantage in the election of state officers. County unit votes were based on population with a minimum of two and a maximum of six per county. Six votes were given to the eight largest counties, four to the next thirty largest, and two to the remainder. If the state had allowed the maximum number to float upwards with the population growth of counties, it would have paralleled exactly the U. S. Electoral College and probably forestalled the later one man-one vote Supreme Court decision regarding state legislatures.

didate "controlled by the fertilizer trust." This was aimed at my father who, besides his many other activities, was also an Armour fertilizer salesman. Blalock's appeal ended any hope my father had of support from the third candidate. There was wild confusion on the floor and it was fully ten minutes before Chairman Harris could restore order and the second ballot could begin. Counties which my father had carried in popular vote began switching to Price.

Harlee Branch, political reporter and later assistant postmaster general under Jim Farley in the Roosevelt administration, was covering the convention for the *Atlanta Journal*. He reported to his readers that "before the second roll call had been more than a third completed it became evident that Price would be victorious."

Papa was the recognized candidate of Thomas E. "Tom" Watson, Populist leader in the 1890's and the party's vice-presidential candidate in 1896, who was known as "the Sage of Hickory Hill," the name he gave his home in Thomson, the county seat of McDuffie County. Watson had endorsed papa in an editorial on February 17, 1912, telling the readers of his *Jeffersonian* weekly newspaper:

> J. J. Brown, of Bowman, would make an ideal Commissioner of Agriculture. He knows all about practical farming; his heart is with the common people; he is perfectly honest, full of energy, a genial mixer, a capital speaker and a good businessman. He is broad-minded and progressive, and at the head of the Agriculture Department, he would be of immense service to the state.

My father had carried McDuffie County in the primary and on the first convention vote received its support, but on the second ballot the delegates from Watson's home county switched to Price. Supporters of the Oconee County candidate cheered wildly, and other delegations began climbing on the Price bandwagon. When it was all over, Price had 214 votes to 141 for Brown.

In the months ahead, as I heard the full story of the Macon Democratic convention, I learned my first lesson in politics: Accept defeat with grace, no matter how it is brought about. Papa needed only a few votes to win on the first ballot, and if the delegates from the counties where he had a plurality at the ballot box had not deserted him, he would have been elected easily. But he made no complaint and took his medicine like a man. After the convention, he made no cry of foul play but returned home to begin the long struggle to recoup his financial losses and to prepare to make the fight for commissioner again.

These events furnished quite a political baptism for a boy of nine. Of course, I was too young then to understand the intricacies of the political process and I could only understand that papa had been robbed by the convention of the office he sought. Nevertheless, I was introduced to the realm of politics and, although I did not realize it at the time, I would shortly find myself in the midst of the political world and remain there through the next half century. And although I did not know it then, many regional and national events took place in 1912 which would shape my life in the years ahead.

In 1912 in Georgia Tom Watson was indicted in federal court in Augusta for sending obscene literature through the mails, and John M. Slaton was elected governor of Georgia with Watson's endorsement. In Baltimore Woodrow Wilson won the Democratic nomination for president after a wild convention in which the Georgia delegation had withheld its support. And over in South Carolina, Senator "Pitchfork Ben" Tillman was re-elected in the same primary in which his supporter James F. Byrnes won a close election to the U. S. House of Representatives from the Aiken district.

All of these men would touch my personal and professional life and draw me into politics and world affairs on the national scene in ways a boy in Georgia could never have imagined would be his lot in life. And although politics had dominated my home life for as long as I could remember, I never dreamed that when my mother told me to go back to bed on that hot Georgia night seventy-odd years ago that I would some day become closely associated with many outstanding and colorful political and public figures.

CHAPTER II

J. J. Brown
Becomes Commissioner
Of Agriculture

The years from 1912 to 1916 were hard for my father. Having had his nomination taken from him by political chicanery at the Macon convention, he was heavily in debt and had no fixed income to fall back on. To his credit, as I have pointed out, he did not sulk in his political tent, but he was deeply hurt. Still, an eternal optimist, he believed in the end the people would right the wrong that had been done.

When James D. Price became agriculture commissioner in 1913, he took over a department that had already become a strong political force in state government. Georgia was then overwhelmingly agrarian, and many governmental agencies—including Statistics, Chemistry, Fertilizer and Oil Inspection, Entomology, Food, Feed, Veterinary and Drugs divisions—were centered in the Department of Agriculture. My father and his friends realized Price, who controlled such extensive patronage, would be next to impossible to defeat in the 1914 Democratic primary. So, following a political strategy devised for the most part by Tom Watson, papa ran against Price in 1914 only to keep what had happened at the 1912 convention fresh in people's minds.

In 1912, Watson had come out full blast for my father. He had criticized the way the department had been run by previous commissioners and had taken the stump to help papa capture the election. Watson again supported papa in 1914, but Price's position was too strong. He totalled 117,734 popular votes and carried 121 of 148 counties for a county unit vote of 312, compared to papa's 80,263 popular and 60 county unit votes.

Thomas E. Watson early in life.

But by the time the 1916 primary rolled around, my father had many factors working in his favor. As president of the Georgia Farmer's Union he had solidified his support in the rural areas which contained the majority of the state's voting power. Since nomination was based on the county unit vote and not the popular vote, a candidate with a rural following had a tremendous advantage; however, the person with the highest unit vote also usually received the largest popular vote.

Thomas E. Watson was born September 5, 1856 a descendant of Scottish and English Quakers who settled in the area in 1760. He was admitted to the Bar in 1877 and began law practice in his home town, Thomson, Georgia (McDuffie County). He was elected to the Georgia House of Representatives in 1882 and before resigning, introduced legislation to reform the convict lease system, alleviate the condition of tenant farmers, fund public education and to restrict and tax operations of railroads and private corporations.

Watson became active in the Southern Farmers' Alliance and was elected to the U.S. House of Representatives in 1890. While in Congress, he introduced the first resolution to authorize rural free mail delivery, as well as bills for direct election of Senators, income taxation of individuals and the eighthour workday, as well as other reform legislation.

Thomas E. Watson when he was
an active Populist.

Opposed by the Democratic Party because of his Farmers' Alliance loyalty, Watson was counted out of his campaign for reelection in 1892, an election in which he carried all but one county in his district and lost that by having almost twice as many votes counted against him in Augusta, Georgia, as there were registered voters in that city. His attempt to regain his seat in 1894 was defeated in an election again marked by substantial vote fraud.

Thomas E. Watson being notified of his nomination for Vice President by the Populist Party—1896.

In 1896 Watson was nominated for Vice President on the Populist Party ticket with William Jennings Bryan as the nominee for President. The Democrats refused such a "fusion" ticket and the Republicans won.

Watson then retired from politics as a serious candidate, although running for President on the Populist ticket in 1904 and 1908 as a protest against the Democratic and Republican parties. His substantial state-wide following in Georgia, Populists, Progressives and the like, his magnificent oratorical skills and trenchant editorials in his weekly newspaper, *The Jeffersonian* and in his monthly *Watson's Magazine*, were so influential that no Governor was elected or reelected in Georgia for the next twenty years without Watson's support.

During this era he resumed a very successful law practice and authored his two-volume *History of France*, biographies of Napoleon, Jefferson and Jackson and other miscellaneous writings.

Thomas E. Watson, Candidate, People's Party for President—1904.

Although during his lifetime he was to hold public office for only a little over five years, Tom Watson dominated the political scene of Georgia for over twenty years and had become a significant national figure as the leader of the Southern Populists. He had continued the Toombs-Stephens heritage of championing agrarianism and died the last intellectual to be elected to state-wide office in Georgia.

Papa's association with Watson also enhanced his election bid. He had become vice-president of the Jeffersonian Publishing Company at Watson's request at a time when he was selling stock to finance his publishing enterprise. Watson had built a modern printing plant near Hickory Hill which not only printed his newspapers and pamphlets, but was also equipped to publish his books. It was an expensive operation and Watson needed additional financial support because a campaign against the influence of the Roman Catholic church had cost him much of his advertising. Papa had by this time become well known throughout Georgia and was a respected businessman as well as politician. Therefore, Watson must have concluded that the name of J. J. Brown would add to the company's appeal in Georgia.

Watson also aided papa's campaign in another aspect. In 1915 the famous Leo Frank case still dominated and influenced Georgia politics. Frank had been tried and convicted in 1913 to die for the murder of a young female worker in his Atlanta pencil factory. After his sentence was commuted to life by Governor Slaton, the people of Georgia were aroused and the case attracted national attention. In August, 1915, Frank had been taken from the state penitentiary and hanged. Watson had devoted his publications to airing the details of the case, to proclaiming Frank's guilt and to a denunciation of Slaton, whose law firm represented Frank and whose decision to commute Frank's sentence went in the face of five appellate court decisions.

Frank, from a prominent New York Jewish family, had come to Atlanta to run a sweat shop pencil factory in which the Franks had an interest. Young girls worked long hours in the factory at pitifully low wages. This factory was an example of what Tom Watson, who was dead set against industrializing the southern states, said would happen if the South turned from an agrarian to an industrial society. Watson's philosophy was entirely different from that of Henry Grady who was calling for a "New South".

Mary Phagan, a young Cobb County girl but living in Atlanta at the time of the murder, had been brutally raped and murdered in Frank's pencil factory on Confederate Memorial Day, Saturday, April 26, 1913. Frank's death sentence was affirmed in five separate appeals to the Georgia Supreme Court and the U.S. Supreme Court. Slaton commuted Frank's sentence to life imprisonment just before his term as governor expired in June 1915, in spite of the contrary decision of the Georgia Pardon and Parole Commission. That August, after being taken from the Milledgeville penitentiary, Frank was driven to a point near the Phagan homeplace in Cobb County where he was hanged. The incident produced much controversial discussion which continues to the present day.[1]

The state of Georgia was severely criticized for this incident, and there were newspaper reports that Watson was being threatened with indictment for inciting the lynching and speculation that he might be tried in a court outside Georgia since no impartial trial could be held in the state. This led to a blistering reply by Watson, who listed the officers of the Jeffersonian Publishing Company and asked why he was being "held solely and personally responsible for a public corporation in which there are many officers equally responsible?" Again, attention was drawn to the close relationship between Tom Watson and J. J. Brown.

---

[1]On March 11, 1986, the Georgia State Board of Pardons and Paroles granted Leo Frank a posthumous pardon. The Board made no attempt to exonerate Frank for the crime nor did it comment on the fact that his case was appealed and confirmed three times by the Georgia Supreme Court and two times by the United States Supreme Court. The pardon merely stated that the state of Georgia failed to protect Frank's life and his chance for further appeal.

I had personally seen the intensity of reactions to the Frank case when in June 1915, I had arrived in Atlanta by train from our farm near Alma the day when it was revealed Frank's sentence was commuted by Governor Slaton. In those days we slept on the seats in the passenger car as best we could, and as the train pulled into Atlanta, I awoke to see a newsboy waving a paper with the banner headline, "SLATON COMMUTES FRANK SENTENCE." When I called this to my father's attention, he was stunned. He had been a friend of Governor Slaton, and on the train that night I had heard him tell some fellow passengers he was certain Slaton would not commute Frank's sentence.

We rushed to the capitol from the Terminal train station to find that a mob of outraged people had gathered. I reached the House chamber, where I had earlier served as a page, and made my way to the well where a kind of kangaroo court was in session with Sheriff Mangum in tow. The quivering sheriff was telling how he had been called by the governor's office the night before and informed of the governor's action and then ordered to speed Frank to the state prison in Milledgeville. The sheriff said all he had done was carry out his duty. He had been up all night and begged to be allowed to go home. Someone yelled to let him go and get him out of the chamber. Several men grabbed the sheriff and escorted him to the Capitol Square entrance, and the last I saw of the sheriff, he was being booted down the steps by members of the wildest mob I ever saw assembled. The National Guard had been called out by Governor Slaton. There was no doubt in my mind that if this crowd could have gotten its hands on Governor Slaton, as they had the sheriff, his treatment would have been many times more severe than that accorded Mangum. Perhaps he would not have escaped with his life.

But while this association was a political asset in the 1916 campaign, it was by no means a dominating factor in papa's nomination as Commissioner of Agriculture. His tireless campaigning, his ability to hold his audiences with humor and his knowledge of the problems of farmers made him an effective campaigner.

J. J. Brown's commission as Commissioner of Agriculture of Georgia, signed by Hugh M. Dorsey, who had been elected Governor in 1917 following his 1913 prosecution of Leo Frank.

In his two previous campaigns and as president of the Farmer's Union, my father had covered Georgia, as he would say, "from Rabun's Gap to Tybee Light." There was not one of the 148 counties in which he did not sway an audience with his oratory. His speeches were long but interspersed with humorous stories, and his audiences always stayed to the end.

In response to a call for inflation in order to raise crop prices by increasing the money supply so there would be more money available to spend, papa often quoted a farmer friend who thought "there should be more money in circulation—with a sprinkling of counterfeit if need be." When addressing agitation for an eight-hour workday for factory workers, papa would tell his farm audiences an eight-hour workday was nothing new—"the farmer has always had an eight-hour schedule—eight hours before dinner and eight hours after." This always brought applause and laughter.

Papa enjoyed telling another story, which was well received by his rural audiences, about a speaker calling for redistribution of the wealth, by taxation or otherwise. After one speech, a listener told him that if this were done, it would only be a short time before the smart money people again concentrated the wealth in their hands. What would he do then? The speaker looked his questioner in the eye and calmly replied, "Why, we'll just redistribute it again."

My father had a following in almost every county which included not only Watson's followers, known as "wool hat boys" and "old Pops," but small town merchants and businessmen as well. An active farmer all his life, he knew the problems of agriculture and his appeal for support was based on what he wanted to do if elected to help those who tilled the soil. His promise to establish a bureau of markets perhaps gained him more support than any other. He pointed to the success that the University of Georgia College of Agriculture and its scientists had in teaching farmers to increase production and "to make four blades of grass grow where one had formerly grown," but nothing had been done to help the farmer market his abundant harvest. Papa reminded the farmer he had to buy in a protected market at prices set by others and sell in an unprotected market at prices fixed by others. Having sold fertilizer and farm machinery, he knew the problems farmers had in financing their operations, and he never lost an opportunity to talk about the high interest rates charged by the city bankers. He often related how he had helped set up the Farmers' Bank of Bowman to overcome this problem.

But the 1916 campaign was not without its personal and heated political overtones. Papa charged Price with establishing "the most infamous political machine Georgia has ever seen" and with using this machine to conduct his campaign for re-election. Price retaliated by charging that my father was not a dirt farmer and had not always acted in the interests of

the small farmers of Georgia. Papa was a little more successful in making his charges against Price stick, and this, combined with his campaign platform, gave him the victory.

Still, as the *Atlanta Constitution* of September 14, 1916,
reported, "the race between Price and Brown for Commissioner of Agriculture was one of the closest and warmest of
the primary, and it was not until late at night that the result
was certain." These results showed that papa received
113,472 popular votes to 100,543 for Price. There was an even
greater spread in the county unit vote, with papa carrying 86
counties for a county unit vote of 212, and Price 62 counties
with 138 county unit votes. At the 1916 Macon convention
there was no skullduggery of the type that had occurred in
1912.

Price resigned in February 1917 and Governor Nat Harris appointed papa to fill the unexpired term. He took over
the affairs of the far-flung Department of Agriculture on February 14, 1917, becoming the eighth commissioner since the
department was established in 1874. His salary was $5,000 a
year, and to our family that was big money. There were campaign debts to be paid, and my father had no difficulty convincing my mother, who was a most prudent woman, that
we should lease the large Victorian home which stood at 113
Capitol Square, across the street from the south entrance of
the capitol in Atlanta, and rent out the extra rooms.

CHAPTER III

My Father— J. J. Brown

Politics was the main topic of conversation around the fire-place or on the wide veranda of our home in Bowman and on the porch of our home on Capitol Square in Atlanta, where we moved after my father was elected commissioner of agriculture in 1916. But it was a long struggle for my father from a one-horse farm in north Georgia to the zenith of his political life as head of one of the state's largest governmental agencies.

Born on December 17, 1865, to Ira and Susan Brown, papa was named John Judson Brown, after a famous Baptist preacher of those days. The Browns were descendants of the northeast Georgia pioneers who had entered the territory and carved farms and small villages out of the wilderness. The lit-tle community where papa grew up was called Fellowship, although Vanna was the name used by the post office and the Southern train depot. Ira Brown ran the Fellowship school, and there "J. J." Brown received what was called a grammar school education, although I doubt whether by today's standards it would be the equivalent of more than the completion of the third grade. In 1885, he married Captora Terressie Ginn, the daughter of Middleton Ginn, who lived in Little Holly Springs. My father was twenty at the time, my mother nineteen. The Ginn family developed the famous Ginn Gray fighting chickens. These fascinated papa, and he passed this fascination on to my brothers, much to my mother's displeasure.

Ginn owned four or five hundred acres of land, and he allowed my mother and father to live in a small log cabin across from Little Holly Springs. My parents were truly people of the soil. Cotton was king, and the boll weevil had not yet swept up out of Mexico and across the South, nor had the red Piedmont land been robbed of its fertility by the overuse of row crops.

In addition to taking care of the housework, mama helped papa with the crops. Together they could pick a bale of cotton a day, and as a result of their long, hard work, they soon had enough money to buy some land where they moved into a larger log cabin. There success continued, and before long they replaced the cabin with a five-room house. Here, my sister Pearl was born in 1888, and my two brothers, James Polk and Sylvester, in 1889 and 1894. Another brother, Kyle, was born in 1892 but lived less than a year. During the early nineties papa continued to farm, but he also started working in Bowman, three miles away, riding his bicycle to clerk in a general mercantile store, which also bought cotton and sold guano.

Although neither of my parents had any formal education except for the few early grades in a one-room schoolhouse, they both eagerly sought knowledge and saw to it that their children were better educated. Around 1895, when Pearl was old enough to go to school, papa moved the family to Bowman. However, my mother was the driving force behind the education process. When she was not running the house, working in the field, gardening, milking, cooking and making butter, she would sit down and find something to read. Her interest in reading rubbed off on her children, and she insisted they all buckle down to their studies.

Throughout his life, papa also worked on furthering his education. He kept a small dictionary in his pocket at all times; and when riding on a train or when he had a few leisure moments, he studied the dictionary until he had acquired a good vocabulary. When he entered politics, he came to be regarded as one of the best stump speakers in Georgia because he could adjust his speaking to fit his audience. He was at his best in front of a rural crowd but also did well when speaking to exclusive businessmen's clubs.

But papa's main interests lay in areas other than education. He expanded his farm operation, buying and renting land and running eight or ten plows. He also started purchasing cotton and for a time worked for the Elberton Oil Mill, selling meal and hulls. By the early 1900s, he and Gordon Ginn, a cousin by marriage, had organized J. J. Brown and Company. In addition to running a general merchandise store, they established the first modern Munger cotton gin and the first roller mill to process wheat into flour in that part of the country. The roller mill and an adjoining corn mill were pulled by a large steam engine. J. J. Brown and Company also organized the Bowman Manufacturing Company, which made fertilizer distributors which eliminated the drudgery of spreading guano by hand through a horn from a sack straddled over the shoulder.

Soon, my father built a home next to the mill and near the Gibson-Mercer Academy, one of the several preparatory schools that Mercer University established in various sections of Georgia. It was in this house that I was born on July 25, 1903. I almost did not remain in this world, for during my infancy I had measles and membranous croup, and everyone gave up hope that I would survive.

Dr. W. A. Johnson, the family physician, decided to fill me with calomel and kerosene on the theory that it would

J. J. Brown home in Bowman, Georgia. Walter Brown was born in home with bannisters and subsequently moved to the house with the porch that overlooked the public well in Bowman.

either kill or cure me. It worked, but this tremendous dose of medicine was always given as the reason John Brown had such a puny baby boy like me. And I was quite unlike papa. He was a powerfully built man of 275 pounds, standing over six feet tall, and he could do more hard labor than any hired hand. My brothers took after him and could whip their weight in wildcats.

Their favorite story, which they never tired of telling, was about papa's whipping the village blacksmith. It seems this tremendous, muscular man got angry when papa told him to be more careful with the fire from his blacksmith shop, which was located near the gin and papa's other property. This led to words, and from there to a fight. Papa knocked out the blacksmith, and when word of the fight spread around Bowman, my brothers made no attempt to restrain their pride.

Because Dr. Johnson's remedy worked, I, the youngest Brown child, survived and was named Walter Johnson Brown. Years later, when I was playing sandlot ball, I told everyone I was named after Walter Johnson, the great Hall of Fame pitcher who was a player with the Washington Senators. This meant a great deal in Bowman because the legendary Tyrus Raymond Cobb was born and reared in Narrows, eight miles up the road, and both of my brothers played baseball with him.

According to my brothers, Ty's father was so opposed to baseball that he refused to let him play and made him stay on the farm and plow. The Royston Club would hire a boy to slip into the field, change clothes with Ty and do the plowing, while Ty put on his uniform and joined the club for the game. Ty always returned by take-out time, and the elder Cobb never knew his son had left his plow.

Although neither the roller mill nor the manufacturing plant worked out, papa continued to be a successful farmer. He disposed of the gin but kept the general store operating. He also was constantly looking for a way to make his fortune in business.

In 1907 papa got involved in a mutual insurance company, sold his home and moved to Atlanta. There he bought a home on South Pryor Street and, as supreme vice-president of the Farmer's Mutual Life Protective Association, he occupied an office in the company's three-room suite in the Fourth National Bank Building near Five Points in downtown Atlanta and across the street from the second Kimball House, completed in 1884, after Hannibal Kimbal's first Atlanta hotel was destroyed by fire in 1883. Supreme president and medical director of the company was H. L. McCrary, Asa C. Brown was supreme secretary and treasurer, and W. C. Pressley was listed as supreme organizer. The company had the novel idea of selling a column of one thousand policies for one dollar per policy. When one of the subscribers died, the others paid his survivors one dollar, providing $1,000 in life insurance. Many such companies were quite successful, but as was so often the case in my father's many enterprises, this one was undercapitalized and did not prosper. My brother Ves was keenly disappointed when papa gave up his offices in the Fourth National Bank Building. From there he had a good view of the fighting chickens, which the owner of the Kimball House kept on the roof of his hotel.

In 1910 we returned to Bowman, by then a village of 500. Bowman is near Beaverdam Creek and on the Elberton-Toccoa Highway, a portion of the old Indian Trail from Savannah to the mountains. This was frontier country in the 1790s. After passing Bowman, the Beaverdam flows into the mighty and historic Savannah River in the southern part of Elbert

County. My mother ran the Gibson-Mercer Academy dormitory where we lived while papa built a large, rambling white house just off the Bowman public square. The center of activity was a covered well at this square, which was bounded on three sides by stores and on the fourth by a road along the Southern Railway line, which was the main road to Elberton, the county seat, and to Royston. The north side had a setback opening, facing the square, where our house was built. Here we had an open view of the goings on until, with my father's help, the Farmers Bank was established to compete with the Bank of Bowman. This partially blocked our view from the front veranda to the public well, but we were still able to see what was happening on most of the square.

By this time, papa had taken to the road selling International farm implements, fertilizer and other products. He also began to dabble in politics. His first political office was mayor of Bowman. Papa would be "in chambers" on mayor's court every Saturday morning. In the summer, chambers consisted of a few chairs and a table sitting in the back of a store yard off the square. Here the town policeman brought in the culprits of the previous week.

One Saturday morning, a policemen brought in a little black boy with whom I played. He had been caught stealing, and I wondered how my father would handle the case. The boy admitted his guilt, and he stood before the big mayor trembling and fearful that he would be sent to be a water boy on the chain gang, as was the custom in those days. Papa began one of his sermonettes, which he was a past master at delivering. He told the boy how wrong it was to take other people's property and warned him that stealing little things would lead to stealing big things and that in the end he would wind up in prison. After the boy promised he would steal no more, the mayor said, "Boy, I am going to let you go free this time, but if you are ever brought before me again, I am going to have a little striped suit made for you just like prisoners on the chain gang wear, and you will have to leave your home and live out there with those men in stripes at the prison camp

and tote them water.'' I don't know who was more relieved—me or my black playmate.

In Bowman we were quite isolated from the outside
world. Times were hard, and as the old saying goes, our
pleasures were simple. Life was bleak, but it would have been
bleaker still without Beaverdam Creek. There were no swimming pools, and this creek, which was within walking distance, was one of the closest places for swimming. Certainly
it provided the best place to get a bath in the summertime; so
when somebody was going to the creek for a bath, he said he
was "going washing." The creek also held several good fishing places. There was no manufacturing in Bowman and the
stream was unpolluted except for the red clay dirt which
washed into it after a heavy rain.

There were also two mill ponds near Bowman. The closest was Teasley's mill pond, about one mile from town, where
we also swam and fished. Here, on mill grinding days, we
watched with fascination as the farmers' corn and wheat were
crushed into meal and flour by the large water-driven mill-
stones. The other, Winn's mill pond, was about four miles
upstream toward Vanna. This mill was more elaborate and
the pond was much larger. It was in this pond that I was bap-
tized into the Bowman Baptist Church during my teenage
years.

Bowman had no modern hygiene or sanitary facilities.
Good houses had a well on the back porch, and to take a bath
one used a large tin washtub. By alternately sitting in a chair
and by standing in the tub, with a little exertion one could get
quite clean. In winter the water had to be heated on the
kitchen wood stove and brought to the tub, which was placed
in the bedroom. No homes had toilet facilities. The backhouse and a Sears-Roebuck catalog, old newspapers, and
sometimes corn cobs took care of the calls of nature.

In our home, we had a "company" room where we kept
a beautiful rosewood set of furniture which papa had bought
while we lived in Atlanta. I was told that it came from the estate of a relative of John C. Calhoun, the great South Carolin-
ian. This, along with a mahogany set of furniture in the parlor,

was the pride and joy of the house. The bedroom furniture in the company room included a chifforobe or dresser with two large drawers which rolled out onto the floor. Each drawer contained a potty. When we were sick, we used this room. It was a godsend not to have to light a lantern to find the way to the backhouse in the middle of the night. When I visited Calvin Coolidge's boyhood home in Vermont a few years ago, I discovered it had a toilet contraption on the porch of the house and a Sears-Roebuck catalog was used for toilet paper, just as we had used in Georgia. Not until we moved to Atlanta after my father was elected commissioner of agriculture do I remember our having a home with bathroom facilities. There our house at 113 Capitol Square, directly across from the south side of the capitol, had a bathroom on each floor with a toilet tank which was released by pulling a chain and a bathtub with feet.

The Southern Railway was the lifeline of Bowman. It was a branch line between Elberton, also served by the Seaboard main line, and Toccoa, served by the Southern main line between Atlanta and Washington. From our side porch I could see the trains come and go, and when the station whistle blew, I took off to the depot. I spent a great deal of time there watching the agent converse with other agents up and down the line by the dot-and-dash of Morse code.

The depot was the communications center of Bowman. Here we kept in touch with the outside world. Here we learned Jess Willard had knocked out Jack Johnson and who had been elected president and governor. I could not help but think back to that depot newscenter when years later, riding on the Canadian Pacific across Canada, I received word that Governor George Wallace had been shot in Maryland in his campaign for president. Thereafter, at almost every stop, I would run to the same type depot ticket office in that wilderness country to learn whether or not the Alabama Governor had survived.

Bowman had two local telephone systems but no long distance service. One system served the people in the town, the other rural areas. For a long time, farmers outside Bowman had no phone service since the telephone company, like the power company in later years, refused to spend the money to put up poles and lines to provide service. Finally, the farmers got together and set up their own exchange to serve rural subscribers. At one time I had a job running the country telephone system at night and it was enjoyable listening in on all the gossip in the area. The switchboard for the rural system finally wound up operating from the upstairs of our house on the square.

The train also brought Costa's ice cream from Athens, the nearest large town and home of the University of Georgia, via a branch of another line which connected with the Southern. I met the one o'clock train and trucked the heavy, ice-packed freezer to the drugstore up the grade and unloaded it at the top of the hill. Next I took off the heavy canvas bag, washed off the freezer and moved it into the store behind the soda fountain. For this I was given an ice cream cone with two dippers. During the summer months that was the most coveted job a boy in Bowman could have.

Some of the jobs I had in Bowman may have been a bit too hard, but they taught me to appreciate the value of a dollar. Whatever money we boys had, we had to earn. I sold bluing, pins and needles, *The Grit, The Saturday Evening Post,* the *Chicago Blade and Ledger,* and almost every other kind of product not available to the rural people in and around Bowman.

Next to the drugstore was the Bowman barbershop where I had a Saturday job shining shoes and sweeping up the place. This was a rough job for a boy not yet in his teens, and one perhaps my parents should not have let me have. Around nightfall, the oldtimers would begin coming in for their haircuts and shaves. Many would be in the bottle. I was often the subject of their attention. Among other things, they paid me to say bad words. Had my parents found this out, I am sure I would have lost that job pronto. There were some compensating factors, however, because you also heard all the gossip. Sometimes the drinkers would get rowdy, but if the situation got out of hand, I could always run home, only a hundred yards away.

One Saturday night a country doctor by the name of Jenkins came over from his farm near Big Holly Springs in Hart County for his haircut and shine. He always drove a beautiful pair of horses, which he tied near the barbershop. He was loaded when he arrived and overloaded when he left. Often he was just poured into his buggy because his horses knew the way home. On this particular Saturday night, Beaverdam Creek was up, and the horses missed the narrow wooden bridge. Before the doctor knew it, he found himself and his team swimming for their lives. Fortunately, they made it to the other shore, buggy and all, but as expected this episode became the talk of the town.

When the last customer had been waited on and the shop was swept up, I, thoroughly worn out, would make my way home where my mother would be waiting to give me a second supper. With great pride she counted the silver coins I put on the bed. I often made as much as two or three dollars, which was a lot of money in those days.

I remember being fascinated by automobiles since I first set eyes on the sleek Maxwell Special papa bought to use in his 1912 campaign. Since he had to scrape around to get money to pay off his campaign debts, the car was discretely parked in a barn back of my brother-in-law's Toccoa house. I had never seen such a beautiful car, with its big brass radiator and headlights and matching accessories. I fell in love with it, and while we were staying in Toccoa with my sister, I would sit for hours behind the steering wheel shifting gears and pretending I was driving. However, we were poorer than ever as a result of the campaign, and papa had to sell his Maxwell and once again use the horse and buggy and the train.

Country doctors were most often the first to own an automobile in a small town like Bowman. When I returned home from Toccoa, I found Dr. Johnson had acquired what we called a "one-lung" Brush automobile. It was a one-seater, two-passenger car, cranked from the side, and—as I recall—

chain driven. I know it was painted red, and, needless to say, it fascinated me. His office was in the Johnson Hotel which he and his wife ran across the railroad from the square. Here traveling men stopped on their visits to Bowman. Whenever I heard Dr. Johnson's Brush crank up, I would tear out to the hotel and follow him around town because I could run as fast as his Brush could travel.

Before the automobile was within the financial reach of my family, I had plenty of experience with the horse and buggy. Papa always kept the very best livestock available. He had a fine buggy horse named Dan, and he would sometimes take me on his trips to Elberton.

I could hardly sleep after I watched him prepare for the trip. In winter, bricks were heated in the fireplace overnight, and in the morning wrapped and placed in the buggy under our heavy mohair lap robe. We left before daylight, and with papa from time to time touching up old Dan with the whip, we made the twelve-mile drive in something over three hours.

Years later, when I flew the Concorde from London to Washington, I wrote my grandchildren about those horse and buggy trips to impress upon them how transportation had changed in my lifetime. I flew the Atlantic Ocean, over 3,000 miles, in less time than it took us to travel between Bowman and Elberton with old Dan.

While papa attended to his business in Elberton, I shopped around for articles not available in Bowman, such as agate marbles. Marble playing was almost as big a game in Bowman as was horseshoe pitching. I would take home several bags of marbles and resell them and other items to my friends. After making my purchases and hanging around the stores in Elberton, I would meet papa back at the livery stable, and we would start our return trip to Bowman.

On the drive between Bowman and Elberton, for the most part we passed through miles and miles of farmlands. But we traveled through Harper, Hard Cash, Dewey Rose and Goss where the Southern train stopped and had depots. These communities had general stores, and some boasted a gin. Much of the road, which managed to cross back and forth over the Southern Railway tracks about every mile, was lined with trees. Papa knew the names of each particular tree and would point them out to me.

Gypsies camped in a patch of woods below Bowman when they made their annual trek to our part of the country. They would bring mules, horses and other things to trade and sell. As a boy, I heard all kinds of stories about these dark-skinned people, and sometimes during the day we would ride our bicycles down to their camp to see how they lived. At times we were bold enough to talk to them; but when night came, we stayed close to our homes because we were told they might kidnap us and take us away with them. Nothing like this ever happened, and so far as I knew they never caused any trouble. However, they were good traders, and from the stories I heard they often bested our local people in their livestock deals.

Those trips that I took with papa were forever etched on my mind, and they gave us hours to talk about everything imaginable. They were a major contributing factor for the great love and admiration I held for him. I also loved my mother dearly. It was she who provided the discipline in our household. Fortunately for me then, but perhaps unfortunately in later life, my father would come home on weekends and undo what she had accomplished during the week. She ruled with a peach tree switch which really stung as it was administered to the naked leg. Papa was my protector, and I can remember his holding me above his head where mama could not reach me with her switch.

I loved my father so much that even a mild scold would send me off crying. He loved everything that grew or lived in the woods, especially song birds. Once papa gave me an air rifle but warned me to shoot it only in the woods and not to put anybody's eye out. I was proud of everything I killed with my trusted Daisy rifle and would hurry to show my game to him. One day I killed a mockingbird. When I showed him my prey, he became enraged and shouted and shook me until I was terrified. I ran home and cried my eyes out, but I never again killed a harmless songbird.

When mama and I moved again to Toccoa in 1914 for the birth of my sister's second child, I continued my entrepreneurial activities and developed a real moneymaking venture, and thus earned enough money to buy my first bicycle.

The Southern's most popular passenger train between Atlanta, Washington and New York was #39, later known as the New York-New Orleans or Crescent Limited. The southbound #38 met the northbound #39 at Seneca, South Carolina, a few miles above Toccoa. I arranged to get the early edition *Atlanta Journal* dropped off at Toccoa. I just had time enough to rush from school, pick up the bundle of papers, and yell "Atlanta Journal" to the passengers on train #38 as it stopped in Toccoa heading south. It was the first chance the passengers had to buy an Atlanta paper, and I did a good business. One day my favorite teacher, on whom I had a crush, kept me in after school, and my papers remained unsold at the depot. I pleaded with her to let me go in vain, and I never forgave her for not letting me meet the train. After #38 passed, I usually played around the depot waiting for #29 to come in from Atlanta with the late edition *Atlanta Journal* for which I had an established route. By the time #29 arrived I was starving; and, as the dining car passed, the aroma of cooking steaks almost drove me wild. I resolved that some day I would ride that train through Toccoa and eat one of those steaks. About ten years later when I went to Washington for a job interview as a newspaper reporter, I made a special trip to Atlanta to catch #29 and made my dream of eating a delicious steak while passing through Toccoa come true.

The birth of my sister's first child in 1912 had taught me an unwritten rule regarding childbirth. While awaiting the arrival of my first nephew, I awoke one night and heard my sister hollering with pain. I dashed upstairs and stuck my head in the door to see what was wrong. There was my sister, with mama standing by, giving birth to her first child. Pearl took one look at me and yelled, "Get out of here, Walter!" Consequently, when my second nephew was born, my brother took me down to the Swift Hotel at the depot for the night.

Back in Bowman with my new bicycle, I began looking for other ways to make money. There was no *Atlanta Journal* route, so I had to develop another source of income. At that time all ironing was done by heating a flat iron on the stove or in a fire, a hot and tiresome job. I read about a gasoline iron that had been developed and sent off for one. This iron had a small tank of gasoline which flowed through a valve in the bottom of the iron. When lit, it gave off a very hot flame that made it ideal for ironing and saved the drudgery of heating the flat irons. I rode all over Bowman and the surrounding countryside on my bicycle to demonstrate and take orders for the gasoline iron. I sold a great number, and I always cautioned the purchaser never to light the iron without fastening the top lightly on the small gas tank in order to avoid a fire. Regardless of how much I tried I could not communicate to all my customers the serious ramifications of not properly encasing the gas tank. Invariably some would inadvertently leave the top off and the resultant fire would do serious damage. This slowed my sales, but nevertheless, demand for this new appliance continued until electricity and electric irons came to the area.

When my father became president of the Georgia Farmers' Union in 1914, he was furnished with a Model T Ford. There was already a Model T in Bowman which was parked on the square during the day, and I spent hours going through the motions of driving as I had done with the old Maxwell Special in Toccoa. Finally, papa brought his new Model T home. Across the windshield in big yellow letters were the words "Georgia Farmers' Union." Mama took one look and refused to ride in the car until what she called "that tacky sign" was removed from the windshield.

Soon my brother Ves was teaching me how to drive. When Ves was out of town, papa asked me to drive him on short trips. One day I was driving him to Cannon to make a speech at a farmer's meeting, and, coming back that night, our Model T Ford got in the same deep rut with an oncoming

J. J. Brown, President of Georgia Farmers' Union, with Charles Barrett, President of the National Farmers' Union.

Model T. It was impossible to steer either car out of the rut before we met with a crash. The radius rods were bent, and we had to stay overnight at the home of a friend. I was too young to have been driving, but since the man driving the other Model T had only one arm, nothing was ever said about the accident.

Papa called on me to be his driver more and more, despite my mother's obvious displeasure. My early life in Bowman ended about this time when he pulled me out of school to drive him to the Tom Watson obscenity trial in Augusta in November 1916. By then papa had been elected commissioner of agriculture, and we would soon move to Atlanta where a whole new life would open for me. The Watson trial would furnish me with invaluable knowledge of the judicial process and bring me close to the Watson family.

· CHAPTER IV ·

Thomas E. Watson and the Obscenity Trial

Since I could remember, Tom Watson had been a household name. This was to be expected, since my father was a dyed-in-the-wool Populist in early life, and, of course, a Watsonite all his life. My mother more or less stuck with the Democratic Party. As a boy in Bowman, I heard hours and hours of argument between my parents over this disparity. My mother had a knack of finding out how my father stood on political issues of the day, and she usually carefully took the opposite side. She professed not to like Watson, but I concluded early in life that she was prompted in her opinion not so much by an inward feeling against Watson but just to be on the other side of the political spectrum from papa.

The fat was really thrown into the fire when my father announced he was taking me out of school to drive him from

Bowman to the Watson estate in Thomson and then to Augusta for Watson's second trial for allegedly sending obscene material through the mails. My father said I would learn more on the trip than I could possibly learn in the seventh grade. Mama was livid at the prospect of my studies being halted, even temporarily. As generally was the rule around my house, when papa made a decision he prevailed, and we took off for Thomson in our Model T Ford on November 25, 1916. My father always sat on the front seat with me, and on this trip we had two heavyset Populists on the back seat whom papa had been asked to bring along as bodyguards for Watson at the trial. Several threats against the life of Watson had been made and each of the bodyguards carried a pistol. One was a cousin, Ed Campbell, who had some of my father's flair for politics, and there was no doubt he would have gladly given up his life, if necessary, to defend Watson. This was the kind of loyalty Tom Watson stimulated among his followers in Georgia.

It was then a hard, day-long trip over the dirt roads to Thomson. My father was so anxious to reach Thomson before night that he did not want to stop to answer the call of nature. Finally, after we had traveled about one-half the seventy miles from Bowman to Thomson, Cousin Ed spoke up and said: "J. J., don't you think it's about time we stopped and wrung our hank?" This brought a laugh and finally papa had me stop the car so we could visit the woods.

We arrived at Hickory Hill just before dusk, and I will never forget the thrill when I drove up the entrance drive to where the great Sage of Hickory Hill lived. I thought it was the most beautiful place I had ever seen. We approached the side entrance, and papa went in. We were told we were to stay in the old Watson home adjoining the Hickory Hill grounds, about a quarter of a mile down the road toward town. There Watson's daughter, Agnes, who was married to O. S. Lee, lived. "Miss Agnes" was the perfect hostess, and she soon had the Bowman contingent feeling at home and enjoying themselves around a fire in the music, or sitting, room. At the appointed time, a set of sliding doors parted,

Early picture of "Hickory Hill," Senator Watson's home in Thomson, Georgia. This photograph was taken soon after he had acquired the place which was shortly after the turn of the century. Mr. and Mrs. Watson are at the extreme right. His daughter Agnes is second from the left.

and my eyes beheld a most beautiful room with a spread of silver and food the like of which I had never seen.

One episode took place at supper which my father enjoyed telling for many years. Cousin Ed mistook the cream gravy for milk and poured some from the gravy pitcher in his coffee. Papa tried to make a joke of it, but Miss Agnes saw Cousin Ed's embarrassment and, being the hostess she was, blamed the servants for using the milk pitcher for gravy. She sent it back to the kitchen with the spoiled coffee. Out came a new cup of coffee for Cousin Ed with a cream pitcher and a new gravy bowl, and the meal proceeded. But Cousin Ed's putting gravy in his coffee at Miss Agnes' home was the talk around Bowman for a long time.

After dinner Watson's granddaughter Georgia Lee and her cousin Georgia Watson, both three years younger than I, began enticing me to come outside with them. I was shy and a little frightened in my new environment and preferred to stay by the fire on the pretext I was cold. Then Georgia Lee came back and said they were hauling grandpa's "evidence" in her pony wagon down to the Georgia Railroad depot to be shipped on the night train to Augusta and needed some help. I could not resist this invitation, and soon I was helping to get the evidence to the depot. The excitement of the forthcoming trial was evident not only in the Watson household but in the little town of Thomson. I was trusted to drive the pony wagon with the trial papers to the depot because I was a country boy and knew how to handle horses. It made me feel important to be included in the Watson household's activities.

The next morning we gathered at Hickory Hill to form the caravan to drive Watson to Augusta. There was a lead car, Watson's car was next, and then we followed in our Model T carrying papa, who was indirectly under indictment as vice-president of the Jeffersonian Publishing Company, and the two Elbert County bodyguards. The procession also included a few more cars carrying other members of the trial party.

When Watson walked out of Hickory Hill to get in his car, he shook hands with a few of his friends but lost little time getting under way. I was behind the steering wheel of our car, but I thought he noticed me. This was the first time I had ever seen the legendary Tom Watson. My father was a handsome man, and when he dressed for a political gathering he made a fine impression, but Watson with his erect posture, long grey hair and his tail coat presented a picture that has lived with me through life. To be driving a car with bodyguards to protect the man who had become a legend in Georgia was strong medicine for a thirteen-year-old school boy from Bowman.

In those days it was a two-hour drive on dirt roads to Augusta, 30 miles away. As I remember, we crossed the Georgia Railroad tracks twelve times, and at each crossing I hoped nothing had happened to the evidence we had deposited at the depot the night before.

We arrived at the Plaza Hotel at the corner of Walker Street and Barrett Plaza and checked into our rooms. While the conferences with the lawyers went on, I played around with a football in the park between the hotel and the Federal Courthouse. Watson had his meals in his rooms, and I did not see him again until he came down the next morning (November 27, 1916) to join his escort to the United States Courthouse. It was a short walk, but every step seemed to carry a charge of excitement as we made our way to the courtroom on the second floor. It looked to me to be about a half block long on that day, but when I returned to the same room over 30 years later for a hearing before a commissioner of the Federal Communications Commission on an application I had filed for an Augusta radio station, it seemed about one-third the size I had remembered it at the trial.

I was permitted to stay in the courtroom the entire time except when the discussion turned to the translation of the allegedly obscene Latin passages, which were what the trial was all about. Then all minors had to leave, and despite my efforts not to be seen by the marshal, I was fished out and back to the park with my football I went.

Watson was the center of attention in the packed courtroom. Of course, I kept my eyes glued on him almost all the

time. Brought up as I was, there was no question in my mind
that Watson's arrest and indictment for allegedly sending obscene literature through the mails was brought about by the
influence of his political enemies in Washington and by pressure from the Roman Catholic church. The proceedings
against Watson had begun in 1912, when I was only nine
years of age. When the case was called in October 1913, the
indictment was quashed by Judge Rufus E. Foster because the
prosecution had extracted obscene sections critical of the Roman Catholic hierarchy from Watson's magazine writings.
Judge Foster ruled that the entire text of each article had to
be included.

Watson was indicted again in 1914, but a mistrial was
declared November 30, 1915. The *New York Times* reported the
jury stood ten to two for acquittal. Judge W. W. Lambdin
presided at this trial. The second trial got under way November 27, 1916.

While I was too young to take in all the discussions that
took place around our household, needless to say I had become convinced of two things: the Roman Catholic church
was determined to put Watson in jail and curtail publication
of *Watson's Magazine* and the *Jeffersonian* for attacking some of
its doctrines and practices; and, if he entered prison, my father could well follow since he was vice president of the company that published the Watson magazine and newspaper.

Because of the trial's ramifications, my young mind was
quite alert to everything that went on at the federal courtroom. Once Watson, who handled much of his own defense,
lost his temper and let go an outburst against the prosecution
that hushed the courtroom to such an extent one could have
heard a pin drop.

I also remember the young students the prosecution
brought in to translate the Latin passages upon which the indictment rested. There was no question that what Watson had
printed about priests and nuns and what went on in the
monasteries and in the confession box was obscene by the
standards of the day. The bone of contention, however, was
whether or not the general public could read and understand

the material which was quoted only in the Latin of the sources. The prosecution charged that the average Latin student could read it. The defense contended that only a profound scholar could understand the Latin which would require hours of study to translate into English.

As the students rattled off the translations, I thought of the Latin classes at Gibson-Mercer Academy back home. I had heard my brothers talk about how hard their Latin courses were. They had mentioned that a "jack" which provided the English translation could pass them through their examinations.

When Watson handed the students the book from which he had taken the Latin passages and turned to a different page, they stumbled and mumbled and admitted they could not translate it. It was obvious, even to me, that those students had used a "jack" and had memorized their translations of the obscene passages. This to me was the turning point of the trial.

Years later when I came into possession of the stenographic transcript of the trial, I read it with great interest. The incidents which impressed me so much were as I had remembered them. There was not a session of the trial which was not packed with excitement for me, and the courtroom was charged with such intense feeling that I knew I could never forget a moment of the proceedings.

I remember well the clash between Watson and District Attorney Erle M. Donalson. Throughout the proceedings, Watson tried to discover in his questioning of the government witnesses exactly who had initiated the complaint against him. A. J. Knight, post office inspector at Thomson, testified that the matter had been referred to him by his superior, who had been directed by the chief inspector to investigate, as was the normal procedure. Knight, in seizing that particular issue of the magazine, was acting at the suggestion of Alexander Akerman, the United States district attorney in Macon.

Watson then charged that there was a conspiracy against him and that this plot was "an attempt of the Roman Catholic church to suppress and silence and destroy one Protestant."

At this point Donalson asked that the jury be retired. He and Watson approached the bench.

DONALSON: May it please the Court, Your Honor has ruled repeatedly that all evidence tending to show that the Catholics are behind this prosecution and that they are in effect, as the defendant contends, persecuting this defendant would be irrelevant and immaterial. The defendant, representing himself, repeatedly, in the very teeth of Your Honor's ruling, made highly improper argument before this jury, asserting that he was being persecuted, that the Catholics are behind this, that the government had prosecuted him for five years, and other statements that are improper to go before the jury. I have been very patient, may it please the Court; I have done my utmost so far as I could to have this case conducted properly, but I object to that kind of conduct on the part of the defendant and if he persists in it, I will be forced to ask Your Honor to declare a mistrial.

WATSON: May it please the Court. I am not at all astonished that the District Attorney is ashamed of himself and his case.

DONALSON: I cannot tolerate that.

WATSON: I mean that sir, and I will be responsible to you for what I say. This is an infamous prosecution.

COURT: You will please observe order, sir.

WATSON: Here is the American Federation of Catholic Societies Report. This report is made every year by its official Secretary, Mr. Anthony Mantra, who is the man behind your Inspector Knight. This man Mantra, who attacks President Woodrow Wilson because he would not bow to the Cardinals in Mexican relations, and who says that the Roman Catholic Church is prosecuting Thomas E. Watson—this is the fourth report that he has made about it, and it is infamous, and I am going to fight it till I die. It is a Roman Catholic prosecution, and you know it, sir!

COURT: The court will be obliged, if the defendant becomes unduly excited or loses his temper, to require that he not argue the case at all. The court has to take charge of the proceedings here in the interest of proper procedure.

To say the least, it was hot and heavy in the courtroom. Watson in his writings about the Roman Catholic church sought to draw attention to his contention that he had no personal feelings against any individual Catholic, but that his attack was on the Roman Catholic hierarchy. In addressing his jury he referred to an editorial note which appeared at the beginning of later chapters he published in his magazine.

"I was stating in a most courteous way," he said, "that it was not my purpose to make any attack upon the religious faith of any human being; that was his business, not mine. There was no attack made on the religious faith of any human being; no desire to insult, wound, or offend in any way. That is stated over the caption of every single chapter of that series. It is kept there as standing matter."

The complete disclaimer which appeared above every chapter published by Watson on the Roman Catholic hierarchy read: "For the Roman Catholic who finds happiness in his faith, I have no words of unkindness. Some of my best friends are devout believers in their Holy Father. If anything contained in the series of chapters dealing with the hierarchy causes them pain and alienates their good will, I shall deplore it." This had to have a telling effect on the jury.

While the transcript of the trial indicated that Watson conducted his own defense, he had the good judgment to surround himself with able counsel and the case was well prepared. Sam S. Olive, an Augusta attorney, made a most favorable impression on me. He was cool and sincere and, I suppose as a boy, I enjoyed seeing him work on the Latin students.

Olive skillfully handled the testimony of young Eugene Black, Jr., who later became president of the World Bank.

My friend [Mr. Donalson] says, "What about the effect on these college boys?" Eugene Black had a boy testifying in this case. I knew Eugene. There is not a finer fellow in this country. I knew him before he was married, and it makes me feel old to see his boy a witness in this case. This young man is a grandson of Henry Grady and a splendid student. To get that Latin he had to dig it out, and haggle at it like he was trying to cut a watermelon with a serrated rock. Finally he said, "That is the best I can do." "Well, what do you know about Latin?" "Well, I went through the Pea-

cock School there in Atlanta three or four years ago, and I took
the full course in the University of Georgia. I had seven years of
it, but I can't get anything out of that."

In this way Olive created a picture in the jurors' minds
of sincere but misguided college boys blindly following the
instructions of the district attorney in learning their Latin
translations.

William H. Fleming, Watson's lead counsel, would step
in when Watson let his temper get the best of him and must
have been a stabilizing influence. Others at the defense table
were J. Gordon Jones and Dan A. Clarke.

A parade of defense witnesses, more than twenty-five,
testified not only to Watson's character and standing in his
community but to his ability as an author, citing his *Story of
France, Napoleon, Jefferson* and other works published by Mac-
millan and other highly regarded publishing houses. These
witnesses included ex-Governor Joseph M. Brown, ex-Governor M. B. McDaniel and Judge Horace Holder.

Perhaps the most colorful character witness was the well-
known Georgian Rebecca Latimer Felton, who had known
Watson since 1880. She spoke highly of him as a man and as
an author, saying his *Story of France* had been recognized as
a standard history and was used in French schools.

After only a few questions Mrs. Felton was excused. She
turned and instructed the judge: "Don't excuse me. I have
traveled 440 miles to come down here and look at this crowd
here. I know the people in Georgia and they have known me
for all these years and I love them. I am a patriot, if I am not
anything else. I was going to quiz you a little and let you tell
me what I should say, privileged to say, and ask you to let me
say it, and I would be glad to let you do that, but if you say
you have enough of me. . . . " This brought down the house,
and as she left the stand, many in the crowd started to ap-
plaud.

There were other touches of humor during the trial, with
Watson contributing his share. He could be as charming and
as friendly as any man at times, although he also had such a
temper that most people were fearful in his presence.

Still, his affable side came out several times. At one point he told his famous rape story to illustrate his point that there was more than one to prove something:

> There was a celebrated rape case, and the defendant said the woman had consented, that it was not forced, and he was able to prove that she allowed him to feel her bosom. Robert Toombs, in addressing the jury, is said to have uttered these words: "Gentlemen of the jury, when the breastworks are carried, the entrenchments must soon follow."

The courtroom shook with laughter, at which point Watson turned to the district attorney and asked, "What are you laughing at?"

Throughout the trial, Watson called on his vast knowledge of history and literature in making his point that he was writing in the classic tradition. One of the articles for which he had been indicted concerned a papal decree that the ladies of Seville go to special confessors and tell whether their regular confessor had taken advantage of them. Watson produced three authorities to corroborate his assertion—Dr. Samuel Edgar's 1838 edition of *Fallacies of Popery*, William Hogan's book of testimonials and Dr. William C. Lea's *Sacerdotal Celibacy*.

At other times the defendant quoted passages, which might be considered offensive by some readers, from theologian and Latin scholar Peter Dens, the Bible, Herodotus, Cervantes, Swift, Hallam, Robinson, Froude, Gibbon, Shakespeare, Byron, and More. In many of these classics the author often left more questionable sections in the original Latin.

Watson's main argument, however, was that the schoolboys had invalidated their own testimony by being unable to read from the same Latin text from which he had taken the Latin in question: "Opened at a different place, beginning in the middle of the alphabet, instead of at the top, breaking them in the middle of the lesson, instead of when they had it by rote, perhaps, that very Latin for which this defendant was indicted and which they claimed they had translated, those boys told you they could not translate! It was the identical Latin!"

District Attorney Donalson had performed ably throughout the trial, but he must have been hard put to follow Watson. He started by assuring the jury that he would "have nothing but contempt for any prosecuting attorney who would take advantage of his official position to vent any personal spleen or malice in any case." He personally believed the articles were filthy and obscene and would disturb the young reader, causing lascivious thoughts. If Watson was writing a scholarly work, he must see to it that it was not "disseminated generally through the mails."

However, Donalson's major weakness was his inability to refute the defense's contention that the college students he picked had been the best scholars, had taken plenty of time to work up their translations and had even heard the university professors deliver their translations before they were called to testify. He could merely ask the jury, "Doesn't it strike you as disgusting to know that they can read it?"

Judge Lambdin then gave his charge to the Court. He reviewed the charges. He reread section 211 of the U.S. Penal Code on which Watson had been indicted. He offered definitions for the key words in the code—obscene, lewd, lascivious and filthy. He reminded the jury that as in the previous trial, they had to consider the article as a whole, "just as the reader would consider it."

He added, "if the effect of the article as a whole would be to deprave and corrupt the mind of a person . . . whose mind is open to such influences, or if it excites lustful or sensual desires in him, or if it should be filthy, then the publication would violate the statute."

Judge Lambdin decreed that the Latin must be considered in its context. In that case, the judge asserted, "The purpose of language is to convey thought. Now gentlemen, if by using the Latin language the thought was covered up, and it conveyed no thought to the reader . . . it would not be obscene, because it would have produced no obscene thought in the person."

Finally, he warned them that no one factor could determine the question. Freedom of the press was not an issue. If the publications were obscene, then the defendant must be convicted, despite his good character, motives or intentions.

The case then went to the jury. Its deliberations were short, however, for it returned the next day, December 1, with a verdict of not guilty.

When the jury rendered its verdict the Watson people could hardly contain themselves. My father rushed up to Watson to congratulate him and Watson extended thanks all around. There was a lot of milling around, but Watson was soon escorted to the hotel and little time was lost in getting the caravan organized and back on the road to Hickory Hill.

When we arrived, my father went into the house with Watson; after a short time they came out to the yard together. For the first time, Watson took notice of me and asked me a question or two about school. Apparently, he did not quite approve of papa's taking me away from my studies to drive his car to the trial but he made no mention of it to me.

He gave me "Short Talks to Young Men," a booklet he had written. Written in Dorothy Dix fashion, it told his young followers how to act in public, and I gained a lot from reading it. In his chapter on table manners he told his young readers not to eat peas with a knife, pour coffee into a saucer to cool or make a noise drinking it.

When we left for Bowman I pushed the Model T for all it would make as we were anxious to get home and talk about the trial and Watson's victory. Papa thought mama would be over her madness at my being taken out of school but she was as cool as a cucumber toward him and showed no elation at Watson's being acquitted. I am sure, however, that she was glad the long ordeal was over.

Before leaving Augusta, papa had bought me a brown-checkered mackinaw. These coats were in style at the time, and I wore mine to school with great pride. But a few days later, while playing ball on a field near some Negro homes, a young black boy came out with a duplicate of my mackinaw. I was crestfallen and was the subject of much teasing from my teammates. I never wore the coat again and somehow this experience dampened my enthusiasm for talking about my trip to Thomson and Augusta.

My boyhood admiration for the Sage of Hickory Hill did not wane, even though several years passed before I would again come in close association with Watson and his family.

· CHAPTER V ·

Then Came the War

When my father took the oath of office as Commissioner of Agriculture on February 14, 1917, the nation was within weeks of entering World War I. Although President Woodrow Wilson had campaigned for reelection in 1916 on the grounds that he had kept the country out of the European war, events forced him to alter his stand. On April 6 the United States, following the president's leadership, declared war on Germany.

From the outset of the European conflict, a large number of Southerners had felt that American preparedness plans were just schemes to benefit weapons manufacturers and financial interests. Farm organizations as well as Southern political leaders cautioned against making any warlike gestures which might pull the United States into the fray. But when war began, the South rallied in support of the American effort.

Papa's political mentor Tom Watson was already a political and philosophical enemy of Wilson when the New Jer-

J. J. Brown as Commissioner of Agriculture.

sey governor ran for the presidency in 1912. He had persuaded the Georgia delegation to withhold its support from Wilson in the wild Baltimore Democratic convention in which Champ Clark thought he was manipulated out of the nomination. Watson again opposed Wilson in 1916. Some felt Watson's opposition was a vendetta dating back to Wilson's belittling treatment of the South in his earlier political and historical writings. Others believed it was because of the federal government's continued harassment of Watson and Watsonian publications. In any event, Watson also opposed America's entrance into the war and undertook a court test of the Conscription Act of May 8, 1917. He defended two black men jailed for not registering for the draft, arguing the case before a large open-air crowd in Augusta on August 18. Federal District Judge Emory Speer, who later played a part in the suppression of Watson's newspaper, presided.

Watson reasoned that Congress, by enacting such legislation, had violated states' rights to an independent militia, constitutional provisions against such appropriations for longer than a two-year period, English common law practice that a citizen could not be sent out of the country without his consent and the Thirteenth Amendment which prohibited involuntary servitude. That Watson was going into the teeth of popular sentiment was evident, but still he declared, "Shall I, at my time of life, become an opportunist, a conformist, in order to avoid harsh criticism?" He argued, to no avail, that the masses, especially in rural America, were with him. Not only did he lose out in court, and the subsequent appeal, but his beloved and personal organ, the *Jeffersonian*, was soon barred from the mails by federal mandate because of anti-war statements, and never resumed publication.

Although my father was a close political ally of Tom Watson during the war years, for personal reasons he did not go overboard in opposing Wilson and the war. My oldest brother Polk was caught in the draft. After induction, Polk trained at Camp Gordon outside Atlanta. Since he had been around mules and horses, he was assigned to the 118th Field Artillery, a horse-drawn unit. I visited him at Camp Gordon during the influenza epidemic when soldiers were dying like flies. He survived and after basic training, was transferred with the 118th to Camp Wheeler near Macon to prepare for overseas duty.

I drove my father to Macon for a parade of the military units leaving for Europe. We watched proudly from near the old Dempsey Hotel as my brother came by with Battery C and its well-groomed horses and shining artillery. That night at the staging area, we all had an emotional farewell.

Thus, although my father had no fault to find with Watson's continued attacks on President Wilson and the war effort, he had an official duty and a personal desire to make his full contribution to seeing the Germans defeated as soon as possible.

With Polk in France and near the front lines, our family followed the war with great interest and anxiety. Luckily, the Armistice came before his unit saw battle, but he was close enough to the action to be gassed. A happy family gathered at 113 Capitol Square when Polk arrived home—in full uniform and looking like the kind of soldier who had made Americans proud to fly service star flags.

While all this was going on, papa was striving to get the Department of Agriculture organized and to carry out the promises he had made to Georgia farmers. He did not personally become involved in the battle between Watson and Wilson. Rather, he used his office and his energy to improve Georgia farming conditions and stimulate increased crop production to provide the extra food and fiber needed for the war effort.

Papa was a big-hearted person and easily taken in by anyone with a hard luck story. As soon as he took office some employees came to him with their problems and asked to be kept on the payroll. He knew many of the other employees from his tenure as assistant commissioner in 1912. Furthermore he recognized that a certain number of career people were needed to provide continuity. Therefore, he chose not to use a "broom" to sweep out all the Price people overnight. My father's preference for gradual transition did not sit well with many of his friends, but that was his way of doing business.

The Georgia Department of Agriculture now has its own elaborate building at the corner of Martin Luther King, Jr., Boulevard and Washington Street in Atlanta. In 1917, however, a church stood on this corner, directly across from the capitol. The Department of Agriculture for the most part was located on the southeastern section of the first floor of the capitol. The main entrance to the capitol was on Washington Street across from the Presbyterian church. The church property now extends to the north corner of Martin Luther King Boulevard, but in 1917 this area was occupied by the horse-drawn Atlanta Fire Department Sub-Station Number Two. At the south corner of Washington Street was the Second Baptist Church which I attended. Across on Mitchell Street was the Atlanta Girls' High School. Capitol Square, an extension of Mitchell Street, where we lived was residential as was the Capitol Street side of the capitol except for a drugstore. This place was a popular hang-out for state employees, especially those who lived in boarding houses around the capitol.

Papa's office overlooked Capitol Avenue. He had a private entrance from the main floor and a second door led to the chief clerk's office. There Mr. Johnson, with the help of his hunchbacked son, handled the fiscal affairs of the department. Johnson's office also mailed the laboratory results of the fertilizer sample tests which advised farmers of any deficiency in the formula written on or attached to the bags they had purchased. Inspection was made by inserting a long circular tube into the fertilizer and drawing out a small amount to be sent to the department for analysis by the state chemist. His lab in the basement of the capitol under the Department of Agriculture wing and Johnson's office were busy places in the spring when planting time rolled around, fertilizer was moving and both the long- and short-term inspectors were sending in their samples. I had an after-school job in the department and, when not occupied elsewhere, I pitched in to help mail out the reports to the farmers. My job was to look up the county in which each farmer lived from his post office address. This gave me knowledge of the counties in which most towns and cities were located and provided an excellent mailing list.

At one end of the corridor leading to the department wing of the capitol was the office of the state oil inspector. Across the corridor was the office of the assistant commissioner and space for the secretarial people. Here a black janitor, Walter South, would have a roaring coal fire going every cold morning and would shine the shoes of officials who gathered for a morning salutation and discussion. Because of his cheerful personality, he was easily the most popular individual in the department.

Adjoining the assistant commissioner's office were the office of the Bureau of Markets and the Shipping Department. The latter was presided over by a red-headed Cobb County man, Jim Hilburn, whose private office was behind a cage. I had a little desk in the shipping clerk's office, and I will never forget the shock I had when he took me behind his cage and showed me a piece of rope with which he said Leo Frank had been hanged. He was present at the lynching, but

J. J. Brown family on Capitol Square in Atlanta, Georgia. Photographed outside the laboratory of the Department of Agriculture while J. J. Brown was Commissioner:

Left to right: Mr. and Mrs. Carl Teasley (daughter), Mr. and Mrs. J. Polk Brown (son), Walter J. Brown (son), Mr. and Mrs. S. V. Brown (son) and their son, S. V. Brown, Jr., Mr. and Mrs. J. J. Brown, Edgar and Harold Teasley (sons of Mr. and Mrs. Carl Teasley).

he would never talk about it or reveal whether he was on the ride to Milledgeville which brought Frank back to Mary Phagan's home county. Nevertheless, the rope occupied a prominent place on the wall of his office.

When papa took over as commissioner, he immediately brought some new blood into the department. During the 1916 campaign he promised farmers he would set up a marketing system to provide information on crop prices and to assist them with advertising their products. To head this Bureau of Markets, which was established March 1, 1917, fifteen days after he took office, papa named Lemuel B. Jackson. Jackson was not a farmer but worked for a fertilizer company in Atlanta. He had a brilliant mind for organization and administration and he had the Bureau of Markets functioning before the ink on papa's commission was hardly dry.

The first and most important function of the bureau was to establish the *Market Bulletin*, which was distributed free of charge to anyone who asked. In addition to providing the latest market prices, it listed items that farmers wanted to buy or sell.

The *Bulletin* was first printed on a mimeograph machine with typewriter-cut stencils and mailed in hand-addressed or typewritten envelopes. However, as it expanded, multigraph and addressograph equipment were secured, moved into the first floor office, and set up in the Department of Agriculture wing of the capitol to compile, print, and mail the *Bulletin*.

One of my jobs in the department was helping get the *Bulletin* multigraphed and ready for mailing. I would set the type for ads with a picker and transfer the lines of type to multigraph drums from which the *Bulletin* was printed. This made it easier to read than when the *Bulletin* was first printed by mimeograph machine. After running off the desired number of copies, the type had to be knocked down by hand to get ready for the next printing. Addressograph plates bearing the name and address of each subscriber also facilitated the process.

Papa and Jackson soon realized that they had a popular publication on their hands. In 1920, the *Bulletin* was put out for bids for publication by a newspaper plant. The material was then typed in the department and returned in tabloid newspaper format from a Cobb County printing plant. The circulation list was printed on rolls of paper from the metal addressograph plates and professional mailers were brought in to paste on the labels, bundle the publication in proper mailing wrappers, and put the bundles in routed mail sacks. A large room had been provided in the capitol basement, not too far from where Tom Watson's statue now stands, to handle the growing requests for the *Bulletin*.

In 1921, the legislature raised the fertilizer inspection tax from twenty to thirty cents, thus putting Georgia's fee in line with those of neighboring states. This tax, paid by the fertilizer companies, covered the publishing costs of the *Bulletin*. When papa left office in 1927, circulation was almost 60,000 per week, the largest for a publication of its kind in the nation.

As a constitutional officer, my father had keys to the capitol building and in time he let me have one which gave me access at all hours. There was not a crevice or corner in that huge building, from the dome to the basement, that I did not know.

The state library, the state museum and almost every other governmental agency were then located in the capitol building; and it was an education in itself to study the many portraits, statues and museum cases on display. My favorite hangout was the laboratory where in the afternoons after attending Tech High, and later The Georgia Institute of Technology, I spent much of my free time watching the state chemists. They were of much help to me with my studies and several became my close friends. They even let me play in their poker games. Prohibition was in effect but the chemists had access to alcohol which, when added to Coca-Cola, made a drink superior to bootleg corn whiskey and which produced less of a hangover. One chemist was a top-flight golfer and taught me enough about the game to make the golf team at Tech High, the alma mater of Bobby Jones. In those days taking your golf bag by streetcar from the capitol over to the municipal golf course which surrounded the old stockade made you somewhat of an oddity.

The laboratory was built for the most part by plumber and master mechanic John Harris who also was a great fisherman. At his cabin on the Chattahoochee River, he would stage fish fries for papa and special guests, which often included the governor and other prominent politicians. Not only was this retreat great for fishing, but it was also a good place to take girls. I had learned to dance at an Arthur Murray Studio. (Murray attended Georgia Tech and started his career in Atlanta.) I was now really enjoying my new life in the big city of Atlanta—a far cry from the small town of Bowman.

For exercise I often ran up the steps to the capitol dome. On a spring day in 1917 while looking out over Atlanta, I

Fish fry on the Chattahoochee River

Front row: J. J. Brown and Hugh Dorsey are sitting on the front row and Governor Dorsey has two of his children, Hugh Jr. and James, on his lap; and J. J. Brown is holding his grandson, Harold Teasley. Standing to the far left is Dorsey's other son.

Back row: Dr. Brittain, president of Georgia Tech, two chemists, and Walter Brown.

spotted a fire on the North Side. I figured the Washington Street fire department might be called out and I always enjoyed seeing the fire horses move to their positions and charge out pulling the fire trucks. The firemen had been alerted and, as luck would have it, a call came for the station to send trucks to help fight the blaze. I hopped into our Model T and followed to see what was going on. By the time I arrived, the fire had spread and one fireman asked me to drive back to the station to help bring over extra hoses. I thus found myself in the midst of the famous Atlanta fire of May 21, 1917.

I remember that some of the old hose I brought over burst when pressure was applied. In the high wind the flames jumped a block at a time. When the fire passed through the Negro sections, some of the residents rushed into the streets praying and saying the world was coming to an end. The fire raged on, and soon I heard that the mayor and chief of the fire department had given the order to begin dynamiting houses to try to prevent the blaze from spreading. Finally, it was brought under control just before it reached the old baseball park on Ponce de Leon Avenue. But a large section of Atlanta had been burned to the ground. It was a ghastly sight.

When the fire department was motorized, I lost my youthful interest in watching it answer calls but I have always remembered the old fire horses with much affection.

When I first came to Atlanta the governor's mansion was on Peachtree and Cain (now International Boulevard) streets. It was a treat to see the governor leave the mansion to go to the capitol in a carriage pulled by the finest looking horses I had ever seen. I saw those horses replaced by a motor car and eventually saw the old mansion torn down and replaced by the Henry Grady Hotel, which became Georgia's political headquarters. The hotel was run by the Cannon family, who also owned the Scoville Hotel where my father had stayed while in Atlanta before being elected commissioner. The process of change has continued and now the Henry Grady Hotel has been replaced by the ultramodern, circular Peachtree Plaza Hotel. I stayed there when it first opened, but I could hardly sleep for thinking of the days when I saw the governor's horse-drawn carriage leave the mansion and of all the politics I knew had been hatched at the Henry Grady.

The war years greatly affected the agriculture industry in my home state. When the United States entered the war, Georgia and the rest of the South were riding a boom in the cotton market. Prices had risen from seven cents a pound in 1914 to twenty-eight cents three years later, shooting the value of Georgia cotton to $271 million, three times its worth in 1914. Through the efforts of Southern congressmen and farm leaders, the Lever Food and Fuel Control Act of August 10, 1917, made no reference to cotton, although it gave the president authority to: requisition food and fuel for the war effort; purchase, store, and sell wheat, flour, meal, beans, and potatoes; regulate the production of wheat to guarantee its price; control farm implements and fertilizers; and fix the price of coal and coke. It also prohibited the use of foodstuffs in distilled beverages and outlawed hoarding except by farmers' cooperative associations.

In the fall of 1917, papa undertook to organize other state commissioners and presidents of farmers' unions into the Cotton States Official Marketing Board. The board had as its goal better prices and fairer treatment of the cotton farmer and made its influence known not only throughout the South but also in Washington. Papa was its first president and he led a fight in the spring of 1918 against pegging the cotton price at fifteen to twenty cents per pound.

J. J. Brown (third from left, first row) attending cotton conference in New Orleans in 1918.

Out of the nucleus of the Cotton States Marketing Board came a movement led by Harvie Jordan of Georgia and J. Skottewe Wannamaker of South Carolina which resulted in the formation in May 1919 of the American Cotton Association which lobbied in behalf of Southern farmers throughout the 1920s and 1930s.

As soon as papa took office he was appointed by Governor Nat Harris to head a movement to encourage increased production of food crops in Georgia in order to help win the war. Throughout the nation, the federal government, through the newly organized Food Administration under Herbert Hoover, was calling for limited food consumption at home to have more for the fighting forces overseas. Wheatless Mondays and meatless Tuesdays were observed and posters were distributed that read: "Feed a fighter, eat only what you need—waste nothing—that he and his family may have enough." Papa called a state convention of farmers and farm merchants in Macon and began an extensive campaign that resulted in the largest food crop ever produced to that time in Georgia. The wheat and oats crop had been hurt by a severe freeze during the winter of 1917, but Georgia farmers produced record yields in corn, sweet and Irish potatoes, rye and peanuts. With favorable weather in 1918, the state topped previous highs in wheat and oats production as well.

In the summer of 1917, papa and Jackson discovered that yellow Puerto Rican, the sweet potato grown in the South, had been left off the army ration list in favor of the white New England potato. They immediately took up the situation with the quartermaster general in Washington, submitting technical reports on the caloric value and nutritive content of the Puerto Rican juicy yam, which flourished in the southern climate. They received a tart reply that the matter had been settled and the case was closed.

Papa continued to persevere, however, and soon located the source of the problem. My father never was an admirer of Bernard Baruch, whom Wilson selected as chief of war production. He looked upon him as a stock market manipulator who was more sympathetic to the vested capital interests than the welfare of the farmer. Papa had several run-ins with Baruch over decisions affecting the price of cotton and other farm products. When he discovered that Baruch was one of those resisting the movement to have the sweet potato included in the ration list, papa blew sky high. He and other farm leaders rallied friends in Congress and the matter

was carried to President Wilson who recognized that "an un-
just and unwise omission" had been made. The southern-
grown sweet potato was put on the ration list. Soldiers from
all over the United States trained in the South, ate these potatoes and wrote home about them, much as Union soldiers
during the Civil War and Reconstruction had helped to pop-
ularize bright leaf tobacco by writing home about it. Thus
sweet potatoes became an important part of Georgia crop
production.[1]

The success of the movement for increased crop production combined with wartime inflation boosted Georgia crop
values to new highs. In 1916, Georgia farmers produced crops
worth $321 million. By 1918, farm output was valued at over
$783 million.

Throughout his tenure as commissioner, papa remained
concerned about the plight of the small Georgia farmer and
farm worker. In his first annual report to the people in 1917,
he stated that he was "in favor of giving the landless men of
Georgia a better chance to own and operate farm lands of their
own and would like to see legislation . . . to that end." Until
he left office in 1927, he continued to urge the enactment of
a more progressive land tax and tried to find ways to improve
the quality of farm life for the average farmer and farm la-
borer. He wanted to provide better housing, schools, roads,
and churches to the many isolated farm areas. He also wanted
to stop the drain of farm workers to the cities by improving
the financial condition of farmers so that they would be able
to pay higher wages.

At a time when public opinion was being marshalled by
the Federal Committee on Public Information into a campaign
of propaganda against Germany, papa received a lot of criticism for his support of several controversial steps taken by State
Veterinarian Peter F. Bahnsen who was of German descent.

---

[1]While in the White House during World War II, I developed a close association with Baruch—as he was a close friend of James Byrnes and one of his key advisors. I often thought of my father's opinion of him, but never brought the subject
up.

A national movement to prohibit the transporting of tick-infested cattle had begun in the United States as early as 1888, but the Georgia program to eliminate the problem was not started until 1906. Meanwhile state and federal quarantines were established which had the chief effect of discouraging the purchase of cattle without validated health certificates. In 1912 Bahnsen, who took office in 1910, secured state legislative approval of a regulation prohibiting the movement of tick-infested cattle. This regulation was severely criticized because of the time and trouble involved, as was the tick eradication or dipping program. As a result, between 1906 and 1916 only eighteen counties were released from quarantine.

Papa backed up Bahnsen's recommendation that a state-wide tick eradication law should be enacted requiring compulsory dipping. Papa pointed out that cattle would provide food and dairy products for the soldiers in Europe. Bahnsen claimed that the dipping program, which required ten to sixteen dippings in an arsenical solution at fourteen day intervals, could be financed with an appropriation of $100,000 and would be less expensive in the long run than money spent due to disease and delays.

By June 1917 fifty counties were freed from quarantine and by January 1918, seventy. Within three years, 112 Georgia counties were "absolutely tick free," 26 partially so, with 19 still under federal quarantine.

While most farmers and cattle people accepted the cattle-dipping program and the eradication of the blood-sucking tick as not only desirable but necessary if Georgia was going to develop a livestock industry, one prominent Georgian, Tom Watson, opposed the program *in toto*. A big cotton farmer, Watson did not go along completely with plans for diversification of production. His only semblance of farm diversification was growing Tom Watson watermelons for seed. The melon, developed and named for Watson by a friend, not only had delicious sweet red meat, but also a solid rind which made it ideal for shipping to northern markets. He sold the seed by advertising in newspapers. He later turned the seed business over to his brother, W. A. "Top" Watson.

Tom Watson chose not to grow corn because Iowa and the West could produce it cheaper and better and he devoted all his productive land to cotton which could not be grown in the Midwest. Tenant farmers on his vast acreage paid a bale of cotton to the plow[2] and in the fall his massive grove at Hickory Hill was covered with bales of cotton as tenants brought in their rents. I remember seeing a hundred bales scattered in the grove.

Watson had no beef cattle and only a few milk cows but he said that if agents came to take his cattle to be dipped he would be waiting on his porch with his shotgun. When papa heard this, he made a bee-line for Thomson to explain what ridding Georgia of cattle ticks would mean to farmers. Papa was most persuasive in convincing Watson that he should go along with the program. He returned beaming at having brought his political mentor around to accepting a program his department was strongly advocating.

The cattle-dipping program, along with the abolition of the open range in South Georgia when papa was commissioner, laid the groundwork for a cattle industry which now has become an important source of income for Georgia farmers. With the coming of the boll weevil to the South in the 1910s and 1920s, farmers had to find new sources of income. After fighting grass for decades while growing cotton, grass became a friend instead of a foe as herds of cattle grazed in pastures where cotton once grew.

Bahnsen's program for testing cattle for tuberculosis also encountered resistance. Papa again supported his recommendations that the state pay indemnities when it was necessary to kill cattle carrying the disease. The problem was compounded by the importation of cattle with no certificate of health. In 1917, Bahnsen called for a law requiring a certificate of health and a record of a tuberculin test for imported cattle. Then, if the test results looked suspicious, the cattle would be retested. Noting also that only Georgia did not re-

---

[2]A land rental fee of one bale for each mule and plow used.

strict the amount of time animals could be kept on railroad cars without rest, feed and water, he recommended that features of the federal twenty-eight-hour law be enacted. In 1918, he called for the establishment of state and federally recognized tuberculosis-free hands, testing of dairy herds which furnished city milk supplies, and the retesting of all imported cattle. Through his efforts the number of cattle tested for tuberculosis rose each year during papa's tenure.

Bahnsen also wanted a statewide program for production and distribution of hog cholera serum. Here he was at loggerheads with the University of Georgia College of Agriculture. In 1911, Bahnsen had urged the legislature to appropriate $10,000 for distribution of the serum, but he could not get the support of the college which was afraid of jeopardizing its own appropriation bill. The Department of Agriculture had been experimenting with serum production since 1908 and by 1912 Bahnsen believed it could be produced for one cent per cubic centimeter. The college, given the right to manufacture serum for the state, to Bahnsen's consternation charged 2.5 cents. By 1916 the college's production costs were down to one cent, but the program still had not received a federal license. Bahnsen feared that the extra equipment and more extensive testing required for a federal license would again push costs to 2.5 cents. Throughout the war he bought serum both from the college and commercially. The state college criticized the department for this. Bahnsen, citing the cholera serum program, countered that "only by the most reckless mismanagement could serum production cost anyone 2.5 cents."

In order to provide increased service to people who used farm products, papa sent Food Inspector Oscar S. Lee out to explain the new state Pure Food and Drug Law. Lee and his staff stepped up inspection of restaurants and increased the number of samples taken from questionable eating establishments. State Drug Inspector Thomas A. Cheatham expanded his operations and urged legislation requiring that all drugstores be run by properly trained pharmacists. Fertilizer and oil inspection increased as did the fees pouring into the state treasury.

By war's end, the growing department was providing numerous services to most all the people of Georgia. And papa, through his efforts in behalf of the Cotton States Marketing Board, had earned a measure of recognition as a Southern farm leader.

• CHAPTER VI •

Tom Watson:
The War,
Woodrow Wilson
and the Senate

The war had ended happily for the Brown family, but the war years had not been so kind to the Watsons. Personal tragedy caused Tom Watson almost to lose his mind while at the same time pushing him back into politics.

Mrs. Watson had given birth to three children—John Durham in 1880, Agnes Pearce in 1882 and Louise in 1885. Louise, who lived only four years, passed away on April 18, 1889. After attending Agnes Scott College in Atlanta, Georgia, Agnes married widower Oscar S. Lee, a wholesale grocery salesman with two minor sons, Leonard and Stanley. They had one child, Georgia Watson, born March 5, 1906. Watson was most kind to the Lee boys and was like a grandfather to them. Oscar Lee became state food inspector under my father.

Agnes had been experiencing stomach problems for some time and when her condition worsened, doctors began to fear cancer. She was taken to Atlanta for surgery, but the doctors merely sewed her back up and sent her home to die. Ironically, the Georgia Railroad, whose practices Watson had fought, provided a private car for the trip with his daughter back to Thomson. A week after the federal government suppressed *The Jeffersonian,* on August 30, 1917, Agnes died. After her death, Watson began drinking heavily and his health suffered. In January, he moved to his Florida home, as was his annual custom, to forget his sorrows and to enjoy life on the beach where the ocean air helped his asthma.

Watson's only son, John Durham Watson, an intelligent young man who attended school at the Georgia Military Academy at Milledgville, the University of Georgia and studied law for a time in Thomson, Georgia. While in a Long Island, New York hospital John fell in love with a beautiful nurse, Jessie Doremus Millegan. Tom Watson had a difficult time getting along with his Yankee daughter-in-law, but he built a home for his son and daughter-in-law on his property near Hickory Hill. They had one child, Georgia Doremus, born March 27, 1906 in New York where Watson and his son were publishing *Watson's Monthly Magazine.*

Watson at one time owned a three-mile stretch of ocean front at Fort Lauderdale called Las Olas which he replaced with a beach home he built at Hobe Sound on Indian River in Florida. While there to regain his health after Agnes's death, he lost his son, Durham, who suffered from convulsions stemming from a ruptured hernia and died suddenly on April 8. Saddened beyond belief, Watson wired Mrs. Watson the simple message: "Son died in my arms tonight. Get Curtis to arrange funeral."

Las Olas-by-the-sea

WINTER HOME OF THOMAS E.WATSON, 1905-1914, WHERE
HE OWNED 3 MILES OF BEACH FRONT WHICH IS NOW
THE HEART OF FORT LAUDERDALE.

"Losolos"
winter Home of Thos. E. Watson,   Ft. Lauderdale, Fla

*These pictures made of Thomas E. Watson's winter home, where he owned three
miles of beachfront, which is now the heart of Ft. Lauderdale, Florida—1904–1914*

Mrs. Georgia Durham Watson, wife of Thomas E. Watson. Photographed at Hickory Hill prior to Watson's election to the Senate.

Thomas E. Watson at his roller top desk—Hickory Hill.

With all these heart-breaking experiences occurring in rapid succession, added to his long life of political frustrations, Tom Watson became severely depressed and began to drink more and more heavily. The loss of his *Jeffersonian* in 1917 perhaps hurt him most of all.

To keep his mind off his troubles, he was encouraged to enter the 1918 congressional race against Carl Vinson. Few thought he could defeat the popular Tenth District representative, a staunch supporter of President Wilson and American participation in World War I. Watson had represented this district from 1891 to 1893, but was counted out in his bid for reelection by ballot-box chicanery of the worst sort. The district lines of the "Bloody Tenth" had been changed since Watson was elected from the district in 1892, and Vinson's home county of Baldwin had been added, as well as Wilkinson. Getting back into politics did bring new life to Watson and, according to those close to him, caused him to forget his recent troubles and heartbreaks.

The campaign was waged on war issues, with Vinson the war "hawk" and Watson the opponent of American intervention. Vinson attacked Watson by quoting at length from his writings, but Watson did not back down, although he admitted that the war now had to be fought to victory. Rather, he undertook to shift attention to the postwar period, promising if elected, to fight to restore free speech, free press, and individual rights.

When the ballots were counted, Wilson Democrats were shocked because Vinson had carried six counties with a county unit vote of 16, and Watson six counties with a unit vote of 14.

Watson contested the election, pointing to Wilkinson County where Vinson was given the unit vote a week after the results were reported. There were charges of ballot burning. Watson named George Carswell, a state senator, as the manipulator of the votes. The state convention, controlled by Wilson supporters, denied the contest. But Watson was clearly on the way back politically, and he never lost an opportunity to pay his respects to "Ballot Box George."

Soon after the armistice, Watson bought the *Columbia Sentinel*, a weekly published in a county adjoining McDuffie, and he was back in the editorial saddle again, a role he enjoyed more than any other. During this period, I became involved with the Watson family in a personal way.

Oscar Lee had taken a special interest in me and when his daughter Georgia, living at Hickory Hill, visited Atlanta, I was given the opportunity to show her around. We enjoyed each other's company and I was soon invited to visit the Watsons in Thomson. I had not been back to Hickory Hill since I had driven my father to the Augusta trial, and I was no longer the shy lad from Bowman but a teenager from Atlanta who had beén around some. Soon I was on the list for invitations to Hickory Hill.

On one occasion, Georgia Lee and Georgia Watson held a big prom. Japanese lanterns lit the concrete walks around Hickory Hill, and chaperones watched with eagle eyes as we walked through the wooded areas where Watson had planted every kind of tree that would grow in that climate. At ten-minute intervals a bell would ring, and we would hurry back to the big house for another prom with another partner or for lemonade and refreshments. This was my introduction to the social life of Thomson and Hickory Hill.

Although I took my meals at Hickory Hill, I slept at the old Watson home where the Lees had lived. Lee, who had moved to Atlanta after his wife's death, had kept the place just as Miss Agnes had left it.

After the night meal at Hickory Hill and some talk in the large living room adjoining the even larger dining room, I began my long, lonesome walk through the woods to the old Watson home. I knew attempts had been made on Watson's life along this same path and I really lifted my feet up and put them down as I made my way back to the old house at the bottom of the hill. Not a sound was to be heard and it gave me a creepy feeling as I made my way to my bedroom, all alone—a different experience indeed from the night I stayed there on the way to the Augusta trial. I was certainly glad when daylight appeared. The action was on the Hill and, needless to say, I was back there in plenty of time for breakfast.

The main house was a cheerful place. Mrs. Watson had an aviary off the dining room with canaries she raised, singing their hearts out. Watson, who loved birds and built brush piles in the grove to protect them, hated jaybirds because they attacked other birds. He would give me a gun and pay me 25 cents for every jay I killed. Squirrels were everywhere and he advertised in newspapers to obtain different species.

Thomas E. Watson on horseback—Hickory Hill.

Watson stayed in his library working during the daytime except when he came down for a walk in his extensive groves or a ride on his spirited horse. He was an expert horseman. There was plenty of help on the place, and two prize characters were Janie and Horace, a young brother-sister team who did odd jobs around the house. Mrs. Watson had more or less adopted them, and their parents lived and worked on the place. Horace's main job was to keep the coal fires going throughout the house, since there was no central heating.

The Watson plantation was a beehive of activity. There was plenty of livestock around and much to see on the farmstead. It was a life I had read about but had never before enjoyed. The processing of the watermelon seed fascinated me. Melons were brought in from the field and crushed in long troughs erected in back of Hickory Hill. Water from Watson's private water tank was piped into the troughs. Small Negro boys would trounce the bursted watermelons with their feet and the seed would rise to the top of the water. Then they would be floated down to the end of the trough and caught in screened baskets to be dried and made ready for shipment.

Hams and other meats were cured and stored in a smokehouse. A large pigeon house supplied squab, a favorite of Watson's. Watson enjoyed celery, and when it was in season, he would buy it by the crate and bury it in cool earth to preserve as long as possible.

J. C. Cartledge, the overseer for his large cotton farms scattered over the county, also kept the Watson table well supplied with vegetables from a large garden below the main house. "When the leaves on the poplar trees were the size of a squirrel ear," he would begin planting sweet corn. Each two weeks he would plant two additional rows, and he delighted in satisfying Watson's almost daily desire for corn, both on the cob and stewed, from early summer until the first frost.

Cartledge was a loyal friend and an efficient farm manager. He traveled to the Watson farms by horse and buggy to see to it the tenants were properly cultivating the land. Then when fall came, he would see that they paid the "bale a plow" rent.

Mrs. Alice Louise Lytle, Watson's secretary, lived in a cottage back of the main house near the large barn and harness house. In another small cottage near the smokehouse Watson installed a schoolroom in a one-room school house for his two granddaughters' early education. Watson built a long sheetmetal garage especially to house the Apperson Jack Rabbit in which he campaigned in 1918 and 1920.

Watson, who believed in the comforts of home, constructed a large cyprus water tank on top of a 50-foot tower at the rear of his house. A gasoline motor pumped water from a tremendous well in the pasture below the barn, not only to supply his residence but that of his son and his nearby *Jeffersonian* printing plant. He installed running water at Hickory Hill, along with modern bathrooms connected to a sewer system. Also, he set up a Delco gasoline generator plant to provide electricity which replaced an earlier carbide gas lighting arrangement.

Watson could not have been nicer to me when I visited his home, and I had none of the fear of him that others had shown. Of course, I did not know about his drinking habits and outbursts of temper. One night we were waiting for him to come to dinner, or "supper," as we called it. No one dared go upstairs to tell him that he was holding up the meal—not even his granddaughters whom he truly adored. Finally, Mrs. Watson asked me to go upstairs.

I marched upstairs as big as life, rapped on the door, and when Watson in his high-pitched voice asked, "Who is it?" I replied, "Mr. Watson, this is Walter. We are waiting on you for supper downstairs."

He opened the door, and in a most friendly manner said, "Thank you, Walter," and we walked downstairs to the dining room with his hand on my shoulder as though I had done him a favor. I could see the family was relieved, and I never realized until later that I had gone where others feared to tread.

One night at dinner, Watson began talking about papa. Among other things, he said, "You know, your father is the best stump speaker in Georgia except one."

Indignantly, I said, "Who is that?"

Watson just laughed and pointed at himself.

Mr. and Mrs. Watson treated me very kindly during my visits, but I never knew whether they did so because I had been invited by their granddaughter or because my father was their great friend and supporter, although it was probably a bit of both. However, I did know that I returned to Atlanta feeling I had become in some ways a part of the Watson family. My father could not have been more elated.

When 1920 rolled around, the Watson-Brown axis, if it may be called that, was at the height of its power. My father had run unopposed in 1918 and 1920 and, with one or more fertilizer and oil inspectors in almost all the 154 counties, he controlled a powerful political force.

Watson once wrote a provocative essay comparing political loyalties to bubbles on a stream. As currents shifted, the bubbles came together, drifted apart, or broke up entirely. So, too, as political currents changed, politicians likewise shifted their loyalties, and different pairings resulted. Still, with his loyal rural support and the labor vote, Watson held the balance of power in Georgia and had elected and unelected governors and other state officials for at least two decades.

The nature of these changing political alliances was readily apparent in the Georgia presidential and state Democratic primaries of 1920. Wilson's attorney general, A. Mitchell Palmer, had already entered the presidential primary on March 1, but some Wilson people felt that a Georgian should also be in the race. Hugh M. Dorsey, who had successfully prosecuted Leo Frank and had been propelled by Watson into the governor's office in 1916, was a potential candidate; however, he chose not to run.

Then Senator Hoke Smith, who blew hot and cold on the League of Nations, entered the contest on March 24, causing anti-League Senator James A. Reed of Missouri, whom Watson was supporting, to withdraw. Watson was dissatisfied with Smith, and certainly with Palmer. So on March 26, Watson threw his hat into the ring. But, after his loss to Vinson in his own congressional district, he was not given much chance to upset the Democratic machinery in Georgia, controlled for the most part by Clark Howell of the *Atlanta Constitution*, who was supporting Palmer.

There was no question where my father stood. While he had not become involved in Watson's fight with Wilson during the war, he was ready for battle in 1920 against the League of Nations. He even named one of his prize foxhounds "Reed" after the Missouri senator.

Through his *Columbia Sentinel*, Watson had renewed his attacks on the Wilson administration and sentiment began swinging in his direction. Thus, the results of the April 20, 1920, presidential primary showed that Watson had run a surprisingly strong race, had a plurality of the popular vote and had captured the most counties. Palmer, however, received a majority of the county unit or convention votes. Senator Smith, meanwhile, ran a strong third.

	Popular Vote	County Unit Vote
Palmer	48,460	148 (55 counties)
Watson	51,977	132 (56 counties)
Smith	45,568	104 (43 counties)

Then the fireworks began. Watson appealed to the state executive committee that he should have the support of the delegates to the national convention because he had received a plurality of the popular votes. On May 12 the subcommittee investigating the election denied this request, although Chairman James J. Flynt refused to sign the ruling.

That the Palmerites were confident of victory was evident in the headlines of Howell's *Atlanta Constitution,* which on May 18 announced the opening of the "Palmer convention." But the political tides had changed again and Smith, the *Atlanta Journal* publisher who hated Howell with a passion, combined forces with Watson. When he did, Howell and his Wilson-Palmer supporters were overwhelmed.

At the state convention to name delegates to the San Francisco national convention, I was in the gallery in the old Atlanta Theatre near Five Points with my brother Polk, a hot anti-Wilson war veteran. When Tom Watson was escorted down the aisle to take his seat at the head of his delegates, the crowd which packed the theatre cheered wildly. A banner with a well-done portrait of Watson and the slogan: "Free Press—Free Speech—Free People"[1] preceded him.

Watson was unquestionably the dominating figure at the convention. His resolutions against the espionage, sedition and conscription acts were passed, as were those condemning the Wilson administration. When Palmer delegates protested, Watson rose and said: "You can hiss me all you want

---

[1] I have preserved this banner and it now hangs under protective glass in my living room at Hickory Hill.

to, but we've got you whipped and we're going to keep you whipped." Another time he got the floor during discussion of an anti-Wilson proposal and said: "Let there be no mistake about the resolution. It is mine. Its avowed purpose is to criticize the administration." The convention, of course, sent a Watson-Smith delegation to San Francisco.

Nevertheless, the Palmerites found a sympathetic audience at the national convention. On June 26, by a vote of 26-20, the national committee agreed to hear their case, and placed the Palmer delegation on the temporary role by a unanimous vote. On the twenty-ninth, the credentials committee, headed by Howell, seated the Palmer delegation by a vote of 43-4, even after Watson agreed to give them one-third of the Georgia seats. Thus, the Watson-Smith delegation was completely barred from the national convention.

After the presidential primary, Watson could not have resisted the pressure for him to run for the United States Senate against Senator Smith in the regular 1920 Democratic primary had he tried. Although the *Atlanta Journal* was a Smith organ, the newspaper announced Watson's intention to run on July 25. Watson's formal announcement appeared on August 2 in his *Columbia Sentinel.*

Again political currents shifted and Dorsey, who had also broken with Watson, became the Wilson administration's candidate with the support of Howell and the *Constitution.* Watson lost little time in denouncing Dorsey as an ingrate and charged he had stacked the 1918 convention against him after his primary race against Vinson.

Bubbles may have changed in the stream with many other candidates Watson supported, but not with J. J. Brown, who rode with Watson on the campaign trail and encouraged his employees and friends to send Watson to the Senate.

Watson had bought his long Apperson Jack Rabbitt for the campaign. Among the first to join the automobile age, he even drove to his Florida home when that was an almost impossible task. For years my father enjoyed telling about riding in the back seat of this car with Watson from one campaign meeting to another. On one occasion they were behind time and Watson kept urging his black driver Cliff to step on it, although the dirt road they were traveling left a lot to be desired as far as automobile travel was concerned. Suddenly, Cliff ran over a high bump and Watson and papa hit their heads quite hard against the top of the car. When Watson landed in his seat, he immediately shouted, "Damn it, Cliff, I told you not to drive so fast on these rough roads."

After a rigorous day of traveling and speaking, Watson was often subject to severe asthma attacks. My father would then go to the country hotel kitchen, build a fire in the stove, and make a pot of coffee for Watson, which would bring him some relief.

As the campaign progressed, Watson was riding a wave of popularity in Georgia such as he had not enjoyed since his early days as a Populist leader. It was also evident that the race would be between Watson and Dorsey for Smith had vacillated on too many issues.

During this campaign the leaders of the American Legion, loyal to their Commander-in-Chief President Wilson, first sought to become a factor in Georgia politics by supporting Dorsey. Watson, however, muted this opposition by charging that the legion was an organization of officers who had unnecessarily sacrificed rank and file soldiers in the European conflict.

An incident in Buford which led to Watson's jailing toward the end of the campaign solidified Watson's support and assured his election. Long after, I visited the Buford Hotel and recalled the scene because I always felt strongly that he had been framed. Feeling was running high in the campaign and I have often wondered why he chose to stay in a hotel instead of a friend's home. For once word was out that he was there, it was easy for his political opponents to cause him trouble.

The hotel's upstairs rooms on the mezzanine opened onto a hall which overlooked a court lobby. A boisterous card game, organized in the lobby either by design or otherwise, kept the tired 64-year-old campaigner awake. When he asked the players to minimize their noise, they paid no attention.

Watson probably also had had a drink or two in his effort to get some sleep. About midnight he finally lost his temper and, as I was told, threw a water pitcher from the mezzanine onto the card table and let go a stream of profanity. Soon an officer appeared at his room to arrest him. Watson resisted violently but was overpowered and carted off to a slimy cell previously occupied by a drunk whose vomit was still on the floor. In the cool, damp night, only partly clothed, he shivered uncontrollably until two young boys stuffed some blankets through the bars of his cell.

Watson remained in jail until my father and a rescue party arrived from Atlanta to arrange his release. His campaigning was over. All Watson had to do was write about the Buford incarceration, calling it "as barbarous a specimen of Wilsonism as ever occurred in the mine-slave regions of Pennsylvania." Back in the comfort of his home, Watson and his granddaughters royally entertained the two boys who had brought him the blankets.

In the election, Watson received a plurality of the popular vote, but an overwhelming majority of the county unit vote.

	Popular Vote	County Unit Vote
Watson	111,723	247 (102 counties)
Dorsey	72,885	103 (38 counties)
Smith	61,729	34 (14 counties)

In commenting on the election, he stated: "The fight in Georgia, as shown by the very small vote received by Senator Smith, shows that the lines were drawn between the League and its enemies. Our people simply condemn the effort of

Thomas E. Watson just before going to Washington to be sworn in as U. S. Senator—1921.

Woodrow Wilson and a few other usurpers to change our form of government without the consent of the governed."

However, a run-off was required in the governor's race between Tom Hardwick and Cliff Walker. An effort to link Watson and Hardwick together by encouraging votes for the "two Toms" was helpful to Hardwick, but not altogether successful. Hardwick led the ticket, however, with 104,473 votes to 96,623 for Walker. House Speaker John Holder received 40,476 votes and Joseph M. Brown 2,876.

Watson's support was solidly behind Hardwick. In a letter to J. J. Gordy on September 23, he wrote:

> I am intensely interested in the success of Mr. Hardwick in the runoff primary. Mr. Hardwick and I stand for exactly the same principles and Mr. Walker is in direct opposition to those principles. You will seriously hamper me if you elect a governor who is antagonistic to me and who will be in opposition to me and my work in Washington.

With the subsequent victory of Hardwick, the two Toms had fully repudiated Wilson and his League of Nations in Georgia.

With no meaningful opposition in his general election, the new junior senator bided his time at Hickory Hill until Congress convened in March 1921. William J. Harris, elected in 1918, became Georgia's senior senator.

Watson returned to Washington in style in a special Pullman car with his family members and an official party. His friends formed an escort of cars to pick him up at Hickory Hill and take him to the Thomson depot. After addressing his fellow townsmen, he boarded his private car and rode to Augusta on the Georgia Railroad where the car was attached to a Southern Railway train. On the trip, Watson closeted himself in a drawing room and left all the details of arranging meals and tipping to his old friend Charles McGregor. A family member joked that, by the time the train reached Washington, the porters did not know whether Major McGregor or Watson was the new Georgia senator.

The Watsons took up residence in the George Washington Inn near the Capitol. It had to be a gratifying experience

Thomas E. Watson escort to Georgia Railroad Station in Thomson en route to Washington to be sworn in as U. S. Senator—March 1921.

for Watson to ascend the steps of the Capitol to take the oath of office as United States Senator on March 4, 1921. He had not been in the halls of Congress since he left the House in 1893.

Thomas E. Watson speaking to crowd who escorted him to Georgia Railroad Station at Thomson, Georgia en route to Washington to take the oath as U. S. Senator.

Thomas E. Watson leaving to take up his duties after being elected to the United States Senate—March 1921.

• CHAPTER VII •

J. J. Brown
Declines to Try
to Succeed Watson

My father had no opposition for commissioner of agriculture in 1918 or in 1920, but in the 1922 primary he was opposed by his old political foe, A. O. Blalock, whose withdrawal at the 1912 convention had paved the way for J. D. Price's nomination. Those political bubbles were again swirling, for Senator Watson and Governor Tom Hardwick had broken again. As a result, the governor put his office behind Blalock, even though my father had vigorously supported the two Toms campaign in 1920.

Soon after Hardwick became governor in 1921, he undertook a campaign against the Ku Klux Klan. As a Klan member, my father had attended some conventions and supported the principles upon which it was founded. In the early 1920s, Klan membership was a fact of life for most successful politicians in the South, as well as in many other states, particularly in the Midwest. No social stigma was attached to Klan membership. Revived in 1915 by Methodist Minister Colonel William J. Simmons, the organization spread rapidly after World War I. Somewhat of a reform movement, it supported the enforcement of Prohibition laws, the protection of society against the corrosive influences of increasingly lax moral codes, law and order and the cleaning up of government. It also offered members the opportunity to express a robust Americanism and to protest the foreign influences which seemed to be changing the then-accepted American way of life. One outgrowth of this latter feeling was the effort to restrict immigration which led to the passage of the National Origins Act in 1924.

Of course the popularity of the Klan following World War I had racial overtones, especially in the South. There Southerners feared that black soldiers returning from overseas after experiencing participation in a racially mixed society would cause trouble. Without a doubt, white supremacy was one of the Klan's cardinal principles, but the Democratic party in the South also supported it. Those who believed otherwise seldom offered for political office. The Ku Klux Klan was a dominating political influence in the South, as well as in the mid-West, in the early 1920s and most successful politicians gravitated into that order.

Governor Hardwick called on the Georgia legislature to force Klan members to unmask when appearing in public. The proposal gained support, and the Klan became an issue in the 1922 campaign. In seeking reelection, Hardwick realized the advantage of cultivating opposition to my father, who was recognized as the foremost political ally of Watson. Watson was now supporting Walker, who had the active support of the Klan, for governor. However, he had made no comment on the commissioner of agriculture race for reasons that were more personal than political.

After Watson moved to Washington, he and my father did not see much of each other and an old secretarial feud at Hickory Hill came into play in the 1922 campaign. At Thomson, Watson's two secretaries, Alice Lytle and Dr. Grace Kirkland, both brilliant, each jealous of the other's influence with Watson, vied to be Watson's favorite. Mrs. Watson talked to my father about the problem. Mrs. Watson wanted them both fired but, in the end, Mrs. Lytle won out and Dr. Kirkland left Thomson and moved to Atlanta. Papa had taken Dr. Kirkland's side and he gave her father a patronage job in the Agriculture Department. Whether this was part of an arrangement to get one of Watson's combatant secretaries away from Hickory Hill, I do not know, but one thing was certain: Papa inherited the lasting enmity of Mrs. Lytle. In Washington, Mrs. Lytle became even closer to Watson and was the unquestioned boss of his office.

Therefore, my father was confronted with a two-pronged dagger to his political future: the coalition of Governor Hardwick and Blalock and the loss of Watson's open support. Papa knew Mrs. Lytle would never forgive him and would lose no opportunity to poison Watson against him.

As the primary campaign developed, legislators supporting Blalock and Hardwick attacked the Department of Agriculture and the first cries against a "Brown political machine" were heard. Blalock, the chief critic of papa's handling of the department, on August 16 in a letter to W. A. Laseuer charged: "There are now on the payroll of this department between four and five hundred employees. In my opinion, if it were cut in half it would not lessen its efficiency." In a campaign flyer, he insisted Brown had been extravagant with department funds. He also charged undue political influence, because the chairman of the agricultural committee of the state House of Representatives had two brothers-in-law on the department payroll. Blalock insisted employees were being used for campaigning, claiming Brown "sent out a letter to the inspectors to 'see' their Representatives and Senators before they left home for the Capitol, as it meant something to them personally."

The campaign became quite bitter, and papa lashed back in a third-person broadside "To the People of Georgia":

> There is a campaign of vituperation, falsehoods and misrepresentations going on against J. J. Brown, Commissioner of Agriculture, originating in Wall Street, New York, coming on down to the little cotton gambler and politician in every little town in Georgia. Why? Because ever since Mr. Brown has been Commissioner, he has fought to keep the cotton in the hands of the producer where they could not get hold of it. This is "the milk in the coconut" and this is the fight on Brown.

Papa also pointed out that the legislative committee which investigated the finances of his department had always given him a clean bill of health. Moreover, he reminded voters that the ever-expanding services offered by the department, such as oversight of the gas and oil industry which had recently developed in Georgia, required more men and money than ever before.

Papa inflicted much damage by charging that Blalock as a bank officer in 1920 had made over $6,000 on a cotton loan transaction with J. R. Adams, a small farmer in his home county. Adams had borrowed $585 on one hundred bales of cotton. Four days later, Blalock sold the cotton at $24\frac{1}{8}$ cents per pound. By the time Adams could repay the loan, cotton was down to $11\frac{1}{4}$ cents. Blalock credited Adams at this price, rather than $24\frac{1}{8}$ cents. To papa, this was proof Blalock wanted the office of commissioner so he could "skin all the farmers as he is trying to skin one of his neighbors."

But whom was Watson supporting? He remained silent in his *Columbia Sentinel* on the Brown-Blalock race, although he was aggressively supporting Walker for governor. Papa was also for Walker, though not openly since he had his own campaign to run.

Meanwhile, O. M. Houser, also a candidate for commissioner, had been trying to associate himself with Watson, claiming Watson had given him his support. Papa thought the time had come to smoke Houser out, because Watson had previously assured my father he would not support any other candidate. Papa sent O. S. Lee to Washington to talk with Watson, who on September 9, four days before the primary, sent a wire to the *Atlanta Journal:*

> No authority for statement that I am supporting Mr. O. M. Houser for Commissioner of Agriculture. Mr. Houser has a letter from me dated several months ago which should have put him on notice that I could not support him. If I were in Georgia on the day of the primary, I would vote for J. J. Brown.
>
> Thos. E. Watson

Deliberate or not, this was the wisest way for Watson to handle his position in the Brown-Blalock race. It left papa out of Watson's bitter fight against Governor Hardwick and cleared up any doubt about Watson's support for papa.

While Walker overwhelmingly defeated Hardwick in the governor's race, Brown won his primary with a popular vote of 103,041 to 86,201 for Blalock and 22,978 for Houser. The governing county-unit vote was more one-sided: Brown, 256; Blalock, 148; and Houser, 8. However, since papa failed to receive a majority of the popular vote, it was noted in political circles that demise of the so-called Brown machine had begun.

Thirteen days after the primary, the news flashed over Georgia that Tom Watson was dead. While his health had gone downhill during the unusually hot Washington summer, he had continued to go to his office and appeared on the Senate floor almost every day until the session ended September 22. The people of Georgia did not know about his serious asthma attacks nor that a nurse had attended him for eight weeks before he died the morning of September 26. Thus, the news of his death surprised and stunned his many followers, including my father.

Mrs. Watson, who had left Washington six weeks earlier to ready Hickory Hill for her husband's return at the session's end, was in ill health also. Although the Watsons had moved from the George Washington Inn to a house in the Maryland suburb of Chevy Chase, she still preferred the quiet comfort of Hickory Hill.

C. Vann Woodward, in *Tom Watson, Agrarian Rebel*, described Watson's death as follows:

> On the night of the twenty-fifth, he suffered a hard attack of bronchitis and asthma. "It's my finish," he said at the beginning of the attack. "I am not afraid of death." He repeated the last sentence once. After a cerebral hemorrhage he died the next morning at two-forty, in the sixty-sixth year of his life.

There was a lot of talk that during his last seizure an improper injection given by a Catholic nurse might have caused his death. This was never substantiated.

On the day of the funeral, I drove papa to Thomson, leaving Atlanta before daylight, but by the time we arrived the town was already crowded with people. We parked as close to Hickory Hill as we could and walked to the Georgia Railroad depot to meet the train bringing the special Pullman with Watson's body to the spot from which he had departed only nineteen months before.

Senator Watson's casket being lowered from a special car brought to Thomson, Georgia's railroad station for the funeral.

Representative Tom Bell, who was on the congressional funeral committee that accompanied the body, described the scene as the funeral train passed through South Carolina and Georgia:

I saw large crowds of people at all the stations with bowed heads and tear-dimmed eyes. In Augusta, where our train was delayed for several minutes, thousands of people were standing, waiting to get a glimpse of their dead chieftain. When we arrivéd in Thomson there was a sea of people, variously estimated from ten to fifteen thousand who had gathered from all parts of the country to pay their last tribute of respect to the man they loved so well. Many had driven long distances and some had traveled all night in order that they might have an opportunity to once more look upon the face of their departed friend . . . several men on the day of the burial told me that, on account of not being able to get rooms in which to rest for the night, they walked the streets of the town until the following morning.

Crowd gathered at Hickory Hill for Senator Watson's funeral.

The casket was brought to Hickory Hill and placed in the living room, which had doors to the east and west grounds. It was opened so that the thousands gathered on the spacious grounds could pass through and pay their last respects to their dead leader. The old wool-hat boys wept uncontrollably as they passed the coffin.

View of crowd for Senator Watson's funeral at Hickory Hill.

Dr. E. J. Forrester, former pastor of the Thomson Baptist Church and Watson's close personal friend, conducted the funeral service from the large open porch on the west side of the house. Watson was laid to his final rest under a large magnolia tree next to his mother and father in the Thomson Cemetery, which adjoined the Watson property at the bottom of the hill. In the same plot were buried his son, John Durham, and his daughter Louise, who had died in infancy. His other daughter Agnes lay a stone's throw away in the Lee plot.

Part of crowd attending funeral of Thomas E. Watson—1922—J. J. Brown near right column of westide porch. Watson's body lay in state, in a hallway between the dining room and the main body of the house.

As dirt fell over the Watson grave, an era in Georgia politics ended and the scramble for his political mantle began. As always happens, no sooner does a senator die than speculation begins as to his successor. Since papa had been renominated and enjoyed tremendous political power, it was obvious he would be mentioned as the logical successor since he had been Watson's political ally of more than thirty years.

In the days that followed, over twenty men, including J. J. Brown, were mentioned as candidates to fill Watson's senate seat. Once Watson was buried, Mrs. Lytle, whose influence with Watson had grown during his tenure in the Senate, began going after papa in the *Columbia Sentinel*, which she, along with Grover Edmondson, continued to run until it folded some months later. She charged papa had held a graveyard conference after the funeral to pick Watson's successor to the Senate. The *Atlanta Georgian* reported that papa

was approached after the funeral by several Watson followers who urged him to run. He replied that he felt it was too
soon after the burial to discuss the situation, not indicating
whether he would campaign for the nomination. Six days
later he announced he would not be a candidate.

I have always attributed papa's failure to seek higher office
to his association with Dr. Kirkland, with whom he had become extremely close after she moved to Atlanta where she
continued her secretarial career and did some writing as Tom
Dolan. When papa talked to me about his decision not to run
for the Senate, he told me he just did not believe that he had
the educational qualifications to succeed Watson. He said he
could better serve the people and the state by continuing as
Commissioner of Agriculture. I concluded it was the hot spot
he put himself in between Mrs. Lytle and Dr. Kirkland that
caused him not to offer. After I became a Washington correspondent and observed members of the United States Senate, I became convinced more than ever that papa could have
become an effective senator.

Three days after the funeral, the Georgia Democratic Executive Committee announced that the Macon convention
scheduled to convene October 4 had been postponed until
after the October 17 special election. Governor-elect Walker
and his followers were furious since they had planned to use
the convention to decide on an opponent for Governor Hardwick, who was gearing up to run for Watson's seat.

To stop the Hardwick boom, over 1,200 Georgians assembled in Macon anyway for what became known as the Walker
convention. My father, one of the leaders, urged consolida-
tion behind one candidate. First he threw his support to
Colonel H. H. Dean of Gainesville, but when this candidacy
gained no momentum, he switched to Walter F. George.
George, who had come to papa's room in the Lanier Hotel,
pledged to carry on the Watson tradition by fighting for the
principles for which the Sage of Hickory Hill had stood. My
father also told me that George was picked because he be-
longed to the Klan. The convention, however, adjourned
without uniting behind one candidate.

George, who had risen from lawyer to solicitor general to Superior Court and State Appellate judge and then to justice of the state Supreme Court, had a tough fight on his hands against Hardwick, still smarting from his defeat by Walker, and Seaborn Wright, a staunch prohibitionist from Rome. John R. Cooper, a Macon attorney, also stayed in until the end, although he only received some 1,100 votes. Judge George H. Howard, a Walker supporter, withdrew late in the race to manage George's campaign.

The George forces effectively used Watson's letters attacking Hardwick and spelling out the reasons for their final breach. According to the late senator, Hardwick had broken every promise he had ever made to the people of Georgia. With the support of the old Watson wool-hat boys, the Klan, Governor-elect Walker, my father and Senator Harris, George won easily:

	Popular Vote	County Unit Vote
George	60,436	318
Hardwick	36,328	80
Wright	12,820	14

In the interim, in early October, Hardwick had appointed Rebecca Latimer Felton to fill Watson's seat until the election could be held. Since it appeared Congress would not convene until her successor had been chosen, Mrs. Felton could only be seated if President Harding called a special session of Congress or if the Senate, when it reconvened on November 20, allowed her to be sworn in before the winner of the special election took his seat.

Mrs. Felton, who died in 1930 at the age of 95, had a reputation as an author, feminist and something of a shrewd politician. The widow of congressman Dr. William H. Felton, she began her political career as her husband's press secretary. But in the 1880s, at age sixty-four, she was accepted a job as a columnist on Hoke Smith's *Atlanta Journal,* a position she held until 1920.

She had not taken sides between George and Hardwick, but George announced that he would like to help her, although he thought it would take a special act of Congress to get her seated. Most senators believed that she had no right to the seat since George had already been elected. But no one dared object so soon after women had been granted the right to vote.[1]

Senator-elect George announced that he would wait a day to present his credentials. On November 20, the Senate recessed out of respect to Watson. On November 21, after the credentials of three other senators were read, Senator Harris rose to present Mrs. Felton, expressing the hope that no one would object. At this point, Senator Thomas Walsh of Montana called for discussion on whether an appointed senator could be seated after a successor had been elected. Fortunately, at that moment the Senate was called to assemble in the house chambers for the president's message to Congress.

When they returned, Walsh insisted that the Felton matter be discussed before any other measures. Surprisingly, he then argued in behalf of her being seated; no one objected and she was sworn in as the first female senator in U.S. history. The next day, with George still waiting to be sworn in, she addressed the Senate.

With the election of George to the Senate and with Walker in the governor's office, my father was in a strong position in 1924. This time he had opposition from George F. Hunnicutt, a state rural school agent and editor of the *Southern Cultivator*.

---

[1] This reminds me of a story Senator "Cotton Tom" Heflin of Alabama used to tell about a colleague in the House of Representatives who made a forceful speech against the women's suffrage amendment. He got so worked up he began to call the female advocates of the amendment some very unflattering names. During a break in the debate as the congressmen gathered in the cloakrooms to discuss the proceedings, Heflin took the representative aside and cautioned, "Listen, you better be careful on this issue. One day public sentiment might change and it's going to hurt you."

The congressman looked Heflin squarely in the eye and with a straight face replied, "Tom, public sentiment can't change any faster than I can."

Hunnicutt charged papa was manipulating the state legislature in an effort to prevent that body from passing any law reducing the size of the Department of Agriculture. His followers also claimed that the department was operating at a budget twice what operating expenses should require. Papa said the first charge was ridiculous and was one he had answered many times before. He refuted the second charge by producing a state auditor's report showing it cost only $288,000 to run the department, not $600,000 as his enemies claimed.

Criticism of the so-called Brown machine continued throughout the campaign, both in the legislature and in some newspapers. However, the Department of Agriculture was functioning well and rendering expanded service to the farmers. Moreover, in 1924, with good weather and an abundant harvest, Georgia crops brought in excess of $100 million more than in 1923. The rural areas gave papa unqualified support, and he won 113 of the 160 counties, receiving a county unit vote of 292 to 120 for Hunnicutt. In popular vote the race was closer, with 123,615 for Brown and 94,350 for Hunnicutt. This was a bit disturbing, for Hunnicutt was the weakest candidate papa had faced.

· CHAPTER VIII ·

Eugene Talmadge Defeats J. J. Brown in 1926

Instead of recognizing that his popular support had declined in the 1924 election and concentrating on the operation of the department, my father began spending more and more time on his 1,200-acre Appling County farm and giving free rein to Fred Bridges, his assistant, and Lem Jackson, director of the Bureau of Markets, in running the Department of Agriculture. It appeared to me that after Watson—with whom papa had been associated politically all his adult life—died, he began to lose interest in politics and turned back to his first love, farming.

In 1925, I married Georgia Watson Lee and took a full-time job in the department. I had plenty of opportunity to see what was going on and soon realized that the office of commissioner of agriculture was being used for inappropriate legislative maneuvering.

Bridges had close ties with Deveraux McClatchey, Sr., Secretary of the Senate, who was connected with the Southern Bell Telephone Company. Bridges had a toll-free long distance telephone on his desk and, in effect, was using the influence of the department to promote the interests of Southern Bell.

With papa more interested in dynamiting stumps on his farm than in running the department, Bridges and Jackson, who headed the J. J. Brown re-election committee, as early as 1922 began demanding campaign contributions from employees of the department, without my father's knowledge, I was sure.

After ten years in office, papa had accumulated political enemies, most of whom were disappointed job seekers. He often said that he had ten applicants for every job, and in making the appointment he made "nine enemies and one ingrate." Bridges and Jackson harnessed this unhappiness and

J. J. Brown enjoys fox hunting.

at some point between the 1924 and 1926 elections decided they were strong enough to throw papa overboard and back another candidate. They settled upon James H. Mills, a Farmers Union president whom papa had befriended.

When papa found out about these dealings, he called Jackson and Bridges into his office and gave them a good cussing out, threatening to throw them both out of his office window. I met Lem Jackson in the hall as he was leaving papa's office, and his face was white as a sheet. For some time afterwards, all my father could talk about was those "double-crossing sons of bitches."

Not only was papa's organization breaking down, various coalitions were forming against him. On August 23, 1926, he charged that outside forces were working for his defeat. These, he said, were the same forces that had worked to steal Georgia's votes away from William Gibbs McAdoo and had thrown them to Al Smith at the 1924 Democratic national convention. Because he had done everything in his power to prevent this, he had incurred the lasting enmity of Smith's supporters in Georgia.

Throughout papa's 1926 campaign, most major newspapers in the state, especially Howell and the *Atlanta Constitution*, opposed him. Papa charged that Howell's opposition dated from the 1924 New York convention when he had refused to use his influence to help Howell retain his post as national committeeman, a position he had held over twenty years. William T. Anderson of the *Macon Telegraph*, who, my father insisted, wanted to become "the political Mussolini" of Georgia, and Julian Harris of the *Columbus Enquirer Sun* also strongly opposed papa.

Still, as the primary approached, my father had one big advantage: there were five other candidates in the field. James H. Mills, John R. Irwin, J. S. Shettlesworth, Charles Stewart and Eugene Talmadge would so badly split the vote that papa knew he would easily be reelected. Then the Talmadge forces decided to narrow the field. Irwin and Shettlesworth were paid their campaign expenses to withdraw. Stewart refused the same offer but later dropped out as a matter of principle rather than accept money. Mills also eventually withdrew, leaving only Brown and Talmadge.

Before 1926, Talmadge was an unknown McRae politician who could not gain office in his home city or county. Twice he had lost races for the state legislature, and his only official position had been as attorney for Telfair County. But the various anti-Brown coalitions, headed by Howell and legislators who wanted papa out of office, settled upon Talmadge anyway, and he soon became my father's major opponent.

Somehow Talmadge fell heir to much of the Watson following, and he paraded as the spokeman for the wool-hat boys. He was as different from Watson as day from night, but his mannerisms on the stump and his campaign style—which he copied from Watson—attracted many Watsonites, whose opposition to papa grew out of the Lytle writings in the *Columbia Sentinel.*

Papa thought he could beat Talmadge simply because the latter lacked qualifications for the office. In addition, most of his employees remained loyal. For example, Tom McRae came to Atlanta from McRae with affidavits showing that his fellow townsman had taken money from the county, could not handle his liquor and had other personal problems.

The Brown organization decided papa could finish Talmadge off in a series of three debates in McRae, Elberton and Dawson. By focusing on the charge that Talmadge was an unsuccessful lawyer and without the credentials of a dirt farmer as the state law required, my father figured he could destroy his opposition on the stump as he had done in previous campaigns. However, as William Anderson notes in his biography of Talmadge, *Wild Man from Sugar Creek,* this turned out to be a mistake since, in debating the man, papa was drawing attention to Talmadge's candidacy and "if the debate was no better than a tie, Gene would have gained notoriety and credence as a candidate."

Political speeches and debates were big events for isolated rural communities in the early part of this century. They were forms not only of communication but also of entertainment. *The Atlanta Constitution* captured the atmosphere surrounding the first Brown-Talmadge debate on August 3 in McRae in an article on August 5:

> Long before the hour of speaking, a crowd assembled in a large grove of pine trees opposite the courthouse. Farmers with their wives and children drove in from the hinterland, riding everything from a mule cart to a limousine. Women wearing sunbonnets and homespun clothes mingled with women wearing the latest fashions of Parisian boulevards. Children waved red, green, and yellow balloons, and munched stick candy as the speakers paced back and forth on the stand. Piles of watermelons were on sale at the outskirts of the crowd, and the demand was heavy. Aged and bearded patriarchs edged closer to the speakers' stand and drank in every word as they pulled contentedly on clay pipes and corn cobs.

Accounts of the debate vary. The *Constitution* favored Talmadge, as did the *Macon Telegraph.* On the other hand, the *Georgian* took papa's side.

Papa spoke first, briefly going over his record. The *Georgian* notes that twice he was interrupted by Anderson, who was standing beside the podium—once to ask a question, a second time when the editor of the *Telegraph* shouted "Hurrah for Talmadge!" The *Constitution* did not mention this. Nor did the *Constitution* corroborate the *Georgian* claim that Papa was also interrupted several times by hecklers hired by Talmadge, was completely drowned out during his summation and could not continue until order was restored.

My father charged Talmadge had gained his appointment as county attorney by assisting a man who had bolted the Democratic party and run as an Independent for county commissioner. He further claimed that Talmadge had unloaded one hundred acres of his land, worth no more than ten dollars an acre, on the county for thirty dollars an acre.

Papa then went in for the kill by attacking Talmadge as not much of a politician or lawyer and certainly not a farmer. The Talmadge farm was owned and run by his wife, "Miss Mitt," who had inherited it from her first husband, while

Gene ran around with the boys and earned a scanty living as a lawyer. Papa hit this theme hard and was set for the final blow. My father planned to get corroboration of Tom Mc-Rae's information from one of the local folks, the respected jurist Max McRae, Tom McRae's uncle. Papa turned to Max McRae, who was sitting on the platform, and asked if he considered Talmadge to be a full-fledged, qualified farmer under the law of Georgia. To my father's shock and astonishment, McRae responded that he most assuredly did. Tom McRae had misinformed papa as to what his uncle would say. At that point, papa flushed and was obviously rocked by this statement by one he considered his friend and supporter.

Having survived this crucial test, Talmadge rose to speak and soon demonstrated he had organized the audience. A number of local citizens came to the rostrum to testify for his candidacy. When Talmadge asked for a show of hands of those who had seen him plow, most hands shot up. His farm foreman told the crowd that he had plowed alongside Gene many times.

Then he turned to papa's record. Talmadge produced sworn statements to the effect that inspectors had been assessed five percent of their salary for the Brown campaign war chest in 1922 and 1924. He had records, he claimed, showing that contributions by employees of the Department of Agriculture totaled $7,933 in 1922 and $6,732 in 1924. He presented documents showing that Fred Bridges had collected money to "fix the legislature" on a 1925 oil distillation bill.

Talmadge also pointed to departmental nepotism, a charge which was particularly damaging because Ves, Polk, and I worked for the department. Papa, an avid beekeeper, had passed his interest on to my brother Ves, who had made studies of bee culture on his own. When the devastating disease "foulbrood" threatened the honey producers, the State Board of Entomology appointed my brother apiary inspector. Polk was serving as a fertilizer inspector. Talmadge had been keying on the number of inspectors in the department and now he zeroed in: "His oldest boy is a fertilizer inspector with the Department! His baby boy has a job in the Atlanta office! So Brown had to find another job for his middle son. And what was that? Why he's the bee inspector!" To most of the rural Georgians that seemed as ridiculous as it sounded. However, Talmadge, as commissioner, did not abolish this position.

Papa had a hard time refuting the various charges. The one that hurt him the most concerned his former assistants. He told the crowd that the "traitors and ingrates" Jackson and Bridges, who had double-crossed him while he was on vacation, had since been fired. Finally, he asked: "Would you believe Lem Jackson under oath? He is a traitor!"

The news of papa's big defeat spread quickly across Georgia. The next debate in Elberton in papa's home county of Elbert on August 12 drew about fifteen hundred persons, the same as at McRae. According to the *Georgian*, again there was some rowdyism among the Talmadgeites. Some seventy-five automobiles had accompanied Talmadge, and when papa began to speak, there was so much heckling he could not continue. Judge Raymond Stapleton, who was presiding, interceded and warned the crowd that there were enough

As Commissioner of Agriculture, J. J. Brown (pictured fourth from the left, first row) was Chairman of the State Board of Entomology. Pictured on the Capitol steps in Atlanta, Georgia.

law enforcement officers present to insure an orderly pro-
ceeding. The heckling subsided.

Talmadge began by pointing out that there were over 400
employees in the department, including 191 oil inspectors,
whom he called "the oily boys," who in reality spent most of
their time campaigning. They were "200 paid jackasses scattered over Georgia. They are sucking teat. Let's don't kick
them away from the teat, but let's cut a lot of teats off!"
shrilled Talmadge.

Then Talmadge criticized some of papa's actions as commissioner. For instance, the department still used the spe-
cific gravity test, which was old and obsolete, for oil
inspection, when the most effective test was distillation. He
claimed papa had on one occasion prevented the adoption of
the distillation test in Georgia. If elected, Talmadge would
also cut off the entomology bureau and remove the drugs di-
vision from the department. He also advocated the removal
of the chemistry department, which he said should be out in
the State College of Agriculture.

My father had heard many of these charges in other
campaigns. When he took the podium, he said that three
times in five years he had assisted in drafting bills calling for
the adoption of the distillation test. However, the bills,
weighed down with amendments in the House of Representatives, were defeated. Talmadge finally had to admit that
papa had indeed tried to secure passage of the distillation bill.

My father termed Talmadge's plan to reduce the number
of fertilizer inspectors by placing them at the ports and fac-
tories ridiculous. He pointed out that Georgia inspectors
could not be placed in fertilizer plants in the states bordering
Georgia. And even if fertilizer inspectors were placed in three
shifts at every port, at every railroad crossing into the state,
and at every factory, then the number of inspectors would
have to be increased, not reduced. Most important, the farmers would be hurt because there would be no way to know
which farmer got which fertilizer.

He then pointed out that there were only six long-term
and forty short-term fertilizer inspectors. The number of

short-term inspectors who worked four months at $83.33 per month plus expenses, had not increased in the ten years he had been in office.

Papa further explained that the gas and oil industry in Georgia was growing by leaps and bounds. Kerosene and gasoline had to be inspected at 600 car delivery tanks in Georgia. The inspectors also had to collect oil and gasoline revenue and compile a record of all gasoline sold. They were not on salaries but were paid commissions fixed by law. "If they don't work, they don't get paid."

Papa then informed the crowd that he had opposed Bill Anderson of the *Telegraph* many times, including when Anderson wanted to import Japanese workers to compete with Georgia farmers. And since Clark Howell had not given loyal support to McAdoo in 1924, the McAdoo supporters had opposed Howell's reelection to the Democratic national committee. Howell had come to papa for help and papa, a loyal McAdoo man, refused. As a result, Howell lost his seat and Major Jack Cohen of the *Atlanta Journal* took his place. Howell immediately began picturing J. J. Brown as the head of a political ring. To my father, this proved Talmadge was merely "the stalking horse for sinister politicians who couldn't control J. J. Brown." Talmadge's election "would strengthen the power of politicians the people have repudiated."

Talmadge reiterated his charges of nepotism and the bee inspector story went over just as big in our home county as it did in Telfair county. In the audience were many of the old Watsonites, who had been true-blue supporters of papa until they were misled by the *Columbia Sentinel* after Watson's death. Some were beekeepers like my father and knew Ves was performing a useful service, but they enjoyed the "political sting" of the story just the same.

To gain advantage in the press coverage of the meeting, I had prepared a statement for papa to hand out before the debate. I had used the word "camouflaged" in telling how Talmadge was concealing his true record in Telfair County. When papa got to this word the pronunciation escaped him. He passed over it, saying it was one of those new words which had come out of the World War. Everyone laughed, but I was deeply embarrassed.

Talmadge drew his greatest laughter by taking up papa's charge he had bolted the Telfair Democratic party. "Just think of old J. J. talking about bolting the Democratic party. You people up here know how he let his hair grow out and went bellowing through the political woods like a bull moose."

The crowd roared as Talmadge told the story in his inimitable style, which was one of his attractions to the wool-hat boys. He was, of course, referring to Theodore Roosevelt's campaign for the presidency in 1912 on the Bull Moose ticket. Being on the Georgia Department party ticket, papa supported the party, but his sympathy was with Teddy. But had Polk made no bones about voting for Roosevelt.

After the debate, I went back to my room in the Samuel Elbert Hotel across from the courthouse grounds, threw down my briefcase on the bed and wept. I knew the man I had idolized for so long was beaten. What hurt most was that I had urged papa to debate Talmadge as Tom McRae recommended. I had believed that papa, with his stump-speaking ability, could drive Talmadge out of the race because of his record. Instead, Talmadge, with his ability to entertain and arouse a crowd, had turned the tables.

The third debate was called off—my father explaining that the exigencies of his office did not permit it. The many anti-Brown newspapers interpreted this as an indication that J. J. Brown was running scared. And the charges made by Talmadge and his followers stuck in people's minds, even though one anti-Brown paper admitted probably not one-half of what had been said about my father was true. Still, that publication, too, wanted J. J. Brown out of office.

But there were points which recommended themselves favorably to my father. His opponents had on past occasions charged corruption; however, audits of the department by governmental and private agencies, at the insistence of the state legislature, always concluded there was "not a misappropriated cent." These investigations had cost taxpayers thousands of dollars.

Expansion of the department under my father had led to increased service to all the people of Georgia. In 1925 alone, the Department of Agriculture had sold 2,686 cars of Georgia produce for $2,089,170. The department's inspectors had examined 16,540 food establishments, 166,500 gallons of kerosene and gasoline, and 55,671 tons of fertilizer. Georgia farmers also received $65,000 to compensate for fertilizer overruns.

But press coverage and the emphasis on a Brown machine tended to obscure the facts. And as papa and the *Georgian* tried to point out, many, if not all, of the defects in the department had been legislated into it and could only be remedied by legislating them out. The nature of Georgia laws required that the pure food administration, oil and fertilizer divisions be under the Department of Agriculture. Thus, if Talmadge were elected, he would have control of this same machine. And, in fact, Talmadge would later make the *Market Bulletin* his political organ until in 1931 the Georgia legislature would bar him from writing in it.

These, then, became the big issues of the campaign: the activities of Jackson and Bridges, which helped shape the picture of a political machine "gone mad" in its thirst for power, and the sheer size of the department as a result of all the legislation since 1874, which had placed the various divisions under the commissioner, adding to the image of a vast, Brown-controlled political empire.

The election produced a landslide for Talmadge.

	Popular Vote	County Unit Vote
Talmadge	123,114	362 (139 counties)
Brown	66,659	52 (21 counties)

The morning after the election, I made a beeline to 113 Capitol Square. Although I had married and was living in Decatur, the old place across from the Department of Agriculture was still home to me. I found papa in his front room just getting up. He was sitting on the edge of his bed in his B.V.D. underwear, looking very tired. He was obviously deeply hurt. After so many endorsements at the ballot box, it was hard for him to accept defeat. He started to put on his socks, then turned to me and said, "Walter, there's just one thing I can't understand."

"What's that, Papa?" I asked.

"The ingratitude of the human race."

Then and there I decided I would never again hold a political job, come what may. I had just turned twenty-three, and fortunately I had not been on the state payroll long enough to make it impossible for me to do something else with my life.

Finally the day came for the new commissioner to be sworn in. We had moved all of our files out of the office and were set to leave at high noon. After taking the oath of office before the governor, Talmadge came over to papa's office with his young son Herman, then fourteen. I was twenty-three, and to see the beam on Herman's face as papa turned the keys over to his father was a heart-bleeding experience for me. But the transfer was friendly, and after some hand-shaking and a few brief remarks, papa and I left side by side.

In the years ahead, Gene Talmadge would become the unquestioned leader of the Tom Watson wool-hat boys and there would be still another shift of the bubbles on the political stream. Papa helped Talmadge in his 1942 and 1946 races for governor. My father retained many friends all over the state and his support was welcomed by most candidates seeking statewide political office. He also helped Tom Linder succeed Talmadge as Commissioner of Agriculture. Because of papa's support, Linder put on the masthead of the *Market Bulletin*, "Established by J. J. Brown, Commissioner of Agriculture, 1917-1927." Nothing could have pleased my father more. After Gene Talmadge's death in 1946, papa became a staunch supporter of his son Herman.

CHAPTER IX

A Reporter's First Story: Al Smith in the South

My father's defeat for Commissioner of Agriculture meant that it was time for me to make my own way in the world.

After several unsuccessful business ventures, my wife and I decided we had no alternative but to move into the old Watson home in Thomson and start our own business. Since my boyhood days when I would order anything I could sell or peddle, I had always been fascinated by the mail order business. My wife had inherited the rights to all of Watson's writings, and a large stock of books was on hand at the time of his death. Dodd-Mead had republished his major works, *Story of France, Napoleon* and *Jefferson,* but there continued to be a wide demand for all of Watson's writings for a number of years after his death, especially those on the Roman Catholic church. So, my wife and I decided to start a mail-order book business, the Tom Watson Book Company.

We also began publication of a monthly magazine, *The Watsonian*, to keep her grandfather's memory alive and to assist in selling the Watson books. We believed that with the book company and the return from the Watson farms, we could keep our heads above water and enjoy life. We were hard at it when 1928 rolled around and the Democratic party nominated Al Smith for president.

With the monthly *Watsonian* to get out, I became seriously interested in writing and discovered that I had more talent and zeal for that than I had for the engineering courses at Georgia Tech. I spent one summer at the Henry Grady School of Journalism at the University of Georgia and Dr. John Drewry in this short time taught me the basic tools of journalism. I also gained experience covering events on the campus for the *Athens Banner*.

Some of my writings in the *Watsonian*, especially those opposing Al Smith, attracted the attention of James S. Vance, who had established *The Followship Forum*, a new fraternal weekly newspaper in Washington. While I was sitting in my office one September afternoon, a Western Union messenger brought me a telegram from Washington which read:

> If you would be interested in covering the South for our paper during the presidential campaign, please come to Washington at our expense to work out arrangement. Advise by wire. James S. Vance, Publisher.

Needless to say, I quickly accepted and arranged to go to Atlanta to catch the Southern main line to Washington. I reserved Pullman space on train #29, the same train from which I received the newspapers for my delivery route when I lived in Toccoa. Vance had given me the opportunity to fulfill one of my boyhood wishes. The thrill I received finally eating a steak and looking out the window at the Toccoa Southern station where as a hungry boy I stood so many long nights waiting for my papers is a satisfying memory I will carry to my grave.

Upon my arrival in Washington, I hurried to Vance's office and publishing plant on Pennsylvania Avenue at the foot of the Capitol surrounded by most of Washington's Chinatown. It did not take long to work out an arrangement. I was to spend a week in each of the Southern states where the Democratic revolt against the Smith-Robinson ticket was the strongest. I would start in Alabama, go to Tennessee and Kentucky, double back through Georgia, skip South Carolina, hit North Carolina and Virginia, and wind up back in Washington a week before the election.

Off I went on a dream assignment to cover the most interesting presidential campaign in the Southern states in many years. The question was, would the solid Democratic South be broken as a result of the Democrats nominating for president a member of Tammany Hall, an avowed wet and a Catholic? That was the story to tell and I was soon on my way to tell it.

There was no question in my employment by Vance that I was to practice "advocacy journalism" in presenting the open rebellion against the Democratic presidential nominee. This was no problem to me because this coincided with my own personal political conclusion that it would be unfortunate for the country if one of Smith's political background and connection were elected president.

Drewry had taught me there was nothing wrong with advocacy journalism if my name was used as the writer of such stories. Although he was the son of an old Tom Watson Populist, I'm sure he would not have approved of the extent to which my writings carried me in covering the South in the 1928 campaign for the militant anti-Smith *Fellowship Forum*.

After an extensive tour of the Southern states, I travelled to Washington to brief Vance on what I had learned.

I told Vance that the solid Democratic South was shattered beyond repair in 1928 and that Herbert Hoover would carry a number of states below the Potomac. We discussed the states he thought the *Forum* should concentrate on by sending additional newspapers there during the last weeks of the campaign. I suggested Alabama because I admired the fight Senator Thomas Heflin was making, and I wanted to see him carry his home state for Hoover in 1928 since he was coming up for reelection in two years.

Naturally I was also interested in my home state. I was outraged at the efforts of the Smith leaders and the Georgia press, who were trying to garner the backing of the old Watson people to make it appear that, were the Sage of Hickory Hill living, he would support Al Smith. We decided I should return to Atlanta and report from there during the final two weeks of the campaign.

Apparently Vance was pleased with my work, and we discussed arrangements which would bring me to Washington permanently. He offered me $50 a week, a generous salary in those days, and proposed to take over the sale of the Watson books and pay my wife and me a percentage of the receipts. He also would fulfill subscriptions to the *Watsonian*.

Of course, I wanted to jump at the chance of a job in Washington, the dream of every newspaperman. I told Vance that I wanted to come but I would have to talk it over with my wife and would give him a decision immediately after the election. He agreed.

When I told Henry McLemore, a Tech High School classmate of mine, about the offer, he advised me not to pass up such an opportunity. He had not been so fortunate. He decided to continue job hunting a few more days, and, if unsuccessful, to move on to New York. I had to tell him that since I would be checking out he would have to make his own living arrangements, but I loaned him some money to get him to New York if he failed to land a job in Washington.

Upon my return to Georgia to give what I thought would be good news to my wife and to wrap up my reports on the election, I found the state seething with hostility between the loyal Democrats and the Hoover supporters.

In my story to the *Forum* on October 20, I reported a "raging torrent of dry Protestantism" against Smith and pointed out that the people of Georgia and other Southern states did not relish voting Republican, but they were going to do so to "save" their party. As one Georgian put it: "We are rock-ribbed Democrats but we are not rock-headed Democrats and we know the only way to save the Democratic party is to drive out the Raskobs and Tammanyites by defeating Smith in the 'Solid South.' "

Both sides were playing the racial issue to the hilt. The regulars distributed thousands of circulars quoting the Senate speeches of Cole Blease of South Carolina attacking Hoover and the Republicans for showing favoritism to blacks in political appointments. Anti-Smith Democrats cited the record of the New York governor and Tammany Hall in their appointment of blacks to high governmental positions.

The Catholic issue had become so strong in the South that Hoover and his campaign manager, Dr. Hubert Work, felt compelled to issue a statement disavowing any opposition to Smith on religious grounds. But they knew well that Smith's Catholicism was at the heart of the Southern revolt and that prohibition was just a side issue.

After covering the Heflin speech, I returned to Thomson where I found my wife and other Watson people up in arms against the Smith organization for claiming her grandfather would be supporting Smith were he still living. I helped them organize a rally to repudiate statements by B. J. Stevens, a local attorney and one-time Watson legal associate, who was making this claim. Feeling was running so high in the little town that two sons of the late Sheriff Clary, a close friend of Watson, came to my office, put two .38 pistols on my desk and told me they were there to see that no harm came to me or to Tom Watson's granddaughter. The rally was held without incident.

I returned to Atlanta and wrote my final pre-election story for the *Forum*. I predicted that the Solid South, which by tradition had given 114 electoral votes to the Democratic nominee, would cast less than 40 votes for Governor Smith—that he would only carry Louisiana, Mississippi, and South Carolina.

While I missed Alabama, Arkansas, and Georgia, which Smith carried, my total electoral vote was not far wrong from the sixty-four he actually received. In Georgia a crazy-quilt ballot did the trick. Smith forces had arranged the ticket so that one mark voted for Smith and the state Democratic slate. But if a voter wanted to cast a ballot against Smith and then vote for the Democratic ticket, it was a very difficult task. He had to scratch out everything down to the first name on the state ticket, then turn the ballot sideways and scratch out three of the four national tickets. Still, a number of counties, including Watson's home county of McDuffie, did go for Hoover. In Alabama, Hoover lost by only 7,000 votes, out of almost 250,000 cast. The result probably would have been closer or even reversed had the vote been fair and free.

The South had not gone Republican entirely, but it had voiced a protest against Al Smith and his brand of democracy. It had also taught the Tammany wing of the party a lesson. But I was sure that in 1932 the Southern people would again be ready to rally around the banner of Jeffersonian democracy as long as it was under new leadership.

After the election I had every reason to be on top of the world. My prognostication that Herbert Hoover would knock the Democratic Solid South into a cocked hat had been borne out by the voters. I had a job in Washington and with it a bailout of our not-so-flourishing magazine and book business. But there was a fly in the ointment: my wife did not want to leave the Watson homestead. My frequent absences from home had created a serious family crisis. But I saw no future personally, professionally or business-wise in Thomson. The farm profit in 1927, after taxes and expenses, was barely over $1,000 for a twenty-plow operation. The magazine and book business picked up some during the campaign, but with the Watson printing plant dismantled and sold as a result of the estate settlement, I saw no chance of duplicating with the Watson collection Elbert Hubbard's success with his Royacrofters series as I had envisioned.

Watson's old overseer, J. H. Cartledge, was working for us and I appealed to my wife to leave him in charge of her property and accompany me to Washington. I even bought a new Chrysler bird's-eye-blue wire-wheel convertible roadster from Harry Sommers in Atlanta to take us to the nation's capital. It was the most eye-catching automobile on the road at that time, but even this did not solve my family problem. So, after Christmas dinner, I bade my wife good-bye and told her if she changed her mind I would welcome her in Washington with open arms. Then I took off in the blue Chrysler with yellow wire wheels.

I arrived at the George Washington Inn late at night. The first thing next morning I went to the District of Columbia Building to buy tags for my new car. When the officer asked me for my registration card, I told him all I had on the car was a pasteboard card saying, "Sold by Harry Sommers, Chrysler dealer, Atlanta, Georgia." I thought the man would explode.

"You mean to tell me you drove that car all the way from Georgia with only a sales tag and you were not stopped?" he asked loudly.

I meekly replied, "Yes," afraid I was in deep trouble on my first day in Washington.

"What in hell kind of police people do you have down there?" he asked.

I muttered some answer which he did not find satisfactory, but after a few more questions he finally issued a tag. With this ordeal over, I made my way back to the Inn, where

Mr. and Mrs. Walter Brown and son, Tom Watson Brown—(photographed while Mr. Brown was a Washington newspaper correspondent).

I immediately arranged to garage the Chrysler since I knew I would be so busy with my new job I would have little time to use it.

I had told Vance that I would report to work on January 1st because I wanted to be sure to get back on his payroll when the new year began. So, bright and early on January 1, 1929, I set out for 339 Pennsylvania Avenue. As I walked by the Capitol and then started down the steps toward my office on the famous avenue that connected the Capitol with the White House and passed the site where fifty-one years later Ronald Reagan would be sworn in as the fortieth president, I felt a thrill that is hard to describe. The view from the Capitol up Pennsylvania Avenue, with the Washington Monument in the background, was not nearly so beautiful as it is now, but it was so impressive to this Georgia cracker that I stopped dead in my tracks and resolved: "Here I drive my stakes and never shall I pull them up." I had seen from the inside the power of the Georgia capitol in Atlanta which was patterned after the nation's Capitol. Now I was in a position to try for the "big league" and I liked what I saw. Pulling up my stakes again a decade later and leaving Washington was the most difficult decision I would ever make.

Vance greeted me cordially. We discussed the election in detail, the plans he had for the *Fellowship Forum* and what my duties would be. He then showed me around the plant. The printing press, the largest piece of machinery I had ever seen, dwarfed the presses Watson had had in his plant in Thomson.

James Vance had started in Alabama as a printer. He became interested in fraternal publications and went to Washington to work for the *New Age*, a Scottish Rite Masonic journal. He told me the Masonic magazine decided not to take advertising and so he started the *Fellowship Forum*, which was dedicated to the same principles as the *New Age*, the pillars of which were separation of church and state and the American system of free public schools. The massive opposition to nomination of Al Smith as the Democratic candidate for the presidency brought the *Forum* into the limelight. It soon became better known as the voice of the Ku Klux Klan rather than as a fraternal paper as Vance had intended. I chose not to align myself with any faction and instead saw my stint with the *Forum* as, hopefully, the stepping stone to greater heights in Washington journalistic circles.

Most of my New Year's Day was spent in this kind of indoctrination. Among other things, Vance told me I was to devote much of my time to spearheading a nation-wide campaign to get Congress to pass a bill setting up a Department of Education under a cabinet secretary.

After discussing my new job, I returned to the Inn to take a few snorts and to listen to the Rose Bowl football game on the radio. It just so happened that my Georgia Tech Yellow Jackets were playing California in Pasadena. I had resolved that some day I would accompany Georgia Tech to the Rose Bowl, but by the time I was financially able to do so Southern teams were no longer invited. I turned on the radio and thought I heard the announcer saying to my consternation that a Georgia Tech player had grabbed a fumble and run across the wrong goal line. However, center Roy Riegels of California in recovering a fumble on the Georgia Tech 25-yard line had veered to his right, bounced off two tackles and somehow got turned around and lost his bearings. Off he went, 75 yards to the California goal line for a safety, giving two points to Georgia Tech. It didn't help this poor fellow at all that the final score was 8 to 7 in favor of Georgia Tech.

Even though the game was quite exciting and featured one of the all-time freak plays in football history, I was feeling a little lonely. Nothing is more depressing than being in a strange city on New Year's Day listening to a football game alone with no one to join you for hog jowls and black-eyed peas. But on January 2, I jumped into my new job with an enthusiasm that only those who love the smell of printer's ink can understand. A few weeks later, my life became more enjoyable because my wife joined me. We took up residence in South Cathedral Mansions on Connecticut Avenue near the National Cathedral School for Girls where she and her cousin had attended school while her grandfather was in the Senate.

Once settled in Washington, I quickly grew to love and admire the physical beauty of the nation's capitol. I also became fascinated with politics and the political intrigues of this interesting city.

The lame-duck amendment had not been passed in 1929, so I had the opportunity to observe the Coolidge administration for two months before Herbert Hoover was inaugurated in March. I had shaken hands and was in a group picture with Coolidge in front of the White House when I attended a meeting there with representatives of the Georgia Department of Agriculture in 1925.

I had heard a lot of stories about Calvin Coolidge's penchant for saying as few words as possible to get his point across. One involved a critical biography of George Washington. Rupert Hughes in a biography of the Father of our Country had been very critical of previous works on the first president and had hacked away at some of the legends which had grown up about Washington, like the stories about his never telling a lie and the episode about cutting down the cherry tree. Many organizations were quite upset about this treatment of one of the founding fathers. The Daughters of the American Revolution sent a committee to see President Coolidge to protest the slurs being made by Hughes against the first president. After hearing them at length, Coolidge got up, walked over to his office widow, drew back the curtains and looked over at the beautiful Washington Monument. Turning back to the protestors he said, "Well, I see it's still there. Good day, ladies."

On March 4, 1929, I saw my first presidential inauguration and I had not missed any subsequent one until ice confined me to our home at Hilton Head for the second inauguration of Ronald Reagan in 1985. I watched President Coolidge and President-elect Hoover ride down Pennsylvana Avenue to Capitol Hill from my office window at the *Forum*. More than 10,000 people marched for two hours past the presidential reviewing stand despite a driving rain.

It was customary after a new president was sworn in on the Capitol plaza for the retiring president to head for his train home and leave all the glory to the incoming chief executive, and Mr. Coolidge followed this procedure. When he got to Union Station there was a tremendous crowd there to see him off. Many of the onlookers gathered around his railroad car and began calling on him to make a speech. The National Broadcasting Company had set up a microphone on the observation car for such an eventuality and an announcer urged Coolidge to say something to the radio audience. The ex-president insisted it was Hoover's day, but his advisors replied, "Mr. President, you should at least go out and make a short talk to these people who had taken the trouble to miss the inaugural parade to come and give you this send-off." Finally, after further prompting, Coolidge got up, walked to the rear platform, looked out at the crowd, waved, leaned into the microphone and said "Good-bye." Then he turned and walked back into his car.

The Washington I had moved to in 1929 was quite different than it is today. In many ways it was a typical Southern city. A few blacks held government jobs but otherwise the nation's capitol was segregated from top to bottom. In those days the area around Seventh and U streets was the hub of activity for blacks living in the district. Soon after I arrived a senator told me a story about a Washington black who died and went to heaven. St. Peter met him at the Pearly Gates and after a few preliminaries asked his new arrival where he wanted to stay. To which came the response: "St. Peter, if it's just the same to you, I'd like to go back to Seventh and U streets."

In 1929 the federal budget was $3.1 billion, and there were 68,000 government workers, most in the downtown area. There were only ten departments with cabinet officers, and the White House easily housed all the people working directly for the president.

The House of Representatives and the Senate each had only one office building. The Supreme Court in 1929 was housed in a chamber between the House and Senate wings of the Capitol. The robing room was across the corridor and on many occasions as I shuttled between the House and Senate, I saw the robed justices going to or leaving the bench, which at one time was in the old Senate chamber. Now the Supreme Court has its own building, built in 1935 across the street from the Capitol.

Thus, official Washington was a much smaller, more accessible place for a beginning reporter than it is today.

• CHAPTER X •

A Reporter's Second Story: The Purge of J. Thomas Heflin

National politics is not confined to the Potomac. Each Washington legislator is elected from his state or district and is both beholden to its constituents and subject to the vagaries of the political homefront. Proof of this dictum and one of the most interesting tales to come out of the Democratic debacle of 1928 was the purge of Senator Tom Heflin of Alabama.

One of the reforms which came out of the Populist movement of the 1890s was the direct popular election of United States senators. Before the adoption of the Seventeenth Amendment in 1913, senators were elected by the state legislatures. The log-rolling, lobbying and offering of bribes by special interest groups during this process became such a national disgrace that finally, after years of political agitation, the amendment was passed. Sponsors of the reform, however, could never have dreamed that in the coming years the election process could still be so corrupted by state party machines that the will of the people might again be circumvented.

Such were the circumstances surrounding the Alabama senatorial election in 1930. And when the case was finally brought before the Senate, that body not only failed to take remedial action, it permitted a seat to be taken away from a senator by political chicanery of the worst sort on the basis of party loyalty. The victim was J. Thomas Heflin, elected to the Senate in 1920 and reelected in 1924 without opposition, after having served eight terms in the House of Representatives.

Southern Democratic solidarity had been broken in 1928 by the cross-over to Hoover and the machine politicians who dominated the state parties were frightened about their future ability to control the party reins. Such h was the case in Alabama, which had been held in the Democratic column by a mere 7,000 votes out of 250,000 cast. Many of the machine "big mules" had also used the party to elect to office candidates who favored the large vested interests, such as the power, steel and coal companies.

I saw Tom Heflin for the first time in 1922 at Watson's funeral. I was only nineteen and I thought, "That's how a Senator should look." Long after many of the younger members of Congress had adopted the less formal attire of the businessman, Heflin refused to change his wardrobe from the traditional black cutaway or morning coat. To this he added a white shirt, a broad black bow tie which he neatly knotted himself, and a wide-brimmed black hat. Hanging around his neck was a black ribbon on which was attached his pince-nez. By the mid-1920s he had made some concessions to current fashion, particularly during the muggy Washington summer months. Then he "blossomed" to full sartorial splendor, according to Jack Bethea of the *Birmingham Post*, foregoing his morning coat and appearing on the Senate floor in ivory white cotton suits woven especially for him by mills at Columbus, Georgia.

Born in 1869, Heflin was the son of an Alabama country doctor who was a rather well-to-do planter. His father was a strict disciplinarian who did not believe in coddling his children or in sparing the rod. So, as a boy, Tom Heflin spent hours behind the hickory handles of a cotton plow. Later he would tell his audiences he had been "raised on hickory" but this early spartan existence stood him well when he entered the grind of campaigning. He attended Southern College in Greensboro, Alabama and Alabama Polytechnic Institute in Auburn. In 1893 he was admitted to the bar and began his practice in Lafayette.

Heflin's major interest soon proved to be politics. An exceptional orator, he held his audiences spellbound with his colorful language and amusing anecdotes. In 1893 he was elected mayor of Lafayette and reelected in 1894. He served as register in chancery from 1894 to 1896, resigning to seek election to the state House of Representatives. He served in the House from 1896 to 1898 and was a member of the state Democratic Executive Committee from 1896 to 1902. That year he was elected secretary of state, serving until May 1, 1904, at which time he resigned to run for Congress to fill the vacancy caused by the death of Representative Charles W. Thompson. Heflin served as a congressman from May 10, 1904 until November 1, 1920. Then he resigned to run for the Senate seat of the deceased John H. Bankhead, Sr. Among his opponents were Governor Emmett O'Neal, former Senator Frank S. White, and former Congressman John W. Abercrombie. Despite this strong opposition, he carried the state. During this time, he acquired the "Cotton Tom" nickname because of his many speeches in support of legislation favorable to the cotton farmer, and his summer dress of cotton clothes.

Tom Watson and Tom Heflin entered the Senate together. I remember, in reading the Senate memorial services after Watson's death, coming across one phrase by the Alabama Senator about Watson which has stuck in my mind. Heflin said: "Mr. Watson's mind was wax to receive and marble to retain." After I married into the family, and as I read Watson's *Story of France, Life of Napoleon, Jefferson, Jackson* and many of his other writings, I always thought how true this description of Watson's intellectual abilities was.

I had renewed my brief acquaintance with Heflin during the 1928 campaign. He knew I had married Georgia Watson Lee and we struck it off well together. Of course, I was representing a weekly newspaper with a national circulation which was dedicated to the same objective as Heflin: the defeat of Al Smith.

Until 1928 Tom Heflin had been an effective speaker in support of the Democratic ticket. His oratorical ability was nationally known and his cloakroom stories were the delight

Thomas E. Watson's library being wagoned to Thomson Railroad Station after being sold for $15,000. William A. Watson, Tom Watson's brother, is standing by the front wagon.

of his colleagues. In early November, 1928, 7,500 people gathered in the Atlanta Municipal Auditorium to hear Senator Heflin deliver an address in support of those bolting Smith. He accused Democrats such as Joe Robinson and Josephus Daniels of sacrificing principles in the name of party loyalty and asked, "What would a Democratic victory gain should the party lose its own soul?" He compared Smith with the passage in the Bible which says, "and the mule passed from under him." When Smith bolted the party platform and sent a telegram denouncing prohibition, then went over into the Republican ranks to select Raskob as party chairman, "The Democratic mule passed from under him!"

In answer to Senator Robinson's claim that the Catholic church was just as American as the Baptist church, the Methodist church or any other Protestant church, Senator Heflin pointed out that those churches were governed by American citizens and no American could ever be the head of the Catholic church. He also condemned the Catholic church's opposition to the American public school system and charged that if the Roman Catholic hierarchy could have its way, there would be no public schools in the United States.

When 1930 rolled around, my publisher had me keeping a close eye on Alabama and on North Carolina, where Senator Furnifold Simmons who also openly disavowed the 1928 Democratic ticket, was up for re-election. Simmons had such seniority and status in the Senate that there was little talk of reading him out of the party, although some party regulars viewed him with the suspicion generally reserved for the worst of "party traitors." However, he was a conservative and had always been considered one friendly to influential Democrats in North Carolina. Also, he was quite elderly and he had not made quite the bitter fight against the Democratic ticket that Heflin had waged. Still, he had to be punished. So, the party machine coalesced behind Josiah W. Bailey to unseat Simmons in the Democratic primary and succeeded. Bailey was editor of the Baptist *Biblical Recorder* and had some personal following, but his main support came from the party leaders who wanted to punish Simmons.

The Democratic party leaders in Alabama were more blunt and underhanded in their scheme. There was open talk of punishing bolters. Responding to these threats, Senator Heflin noted that only in Alabama was the attempt being made to exclude as candidates Democrats who had opposed Smith. He had voted for the state Democratic slate of candidates all his life and had only for the first time in 1928 left the national party to cast his ballot against the Smith-Raskob-Tammany ticket.

As a matter of fact, Heflin until 1928 had been a complete "party" man and was a regular of the regulars. As far back as the Populist era he stood with the Democratic Party when the agrarian movement threatened the "Solid South" as it had not been threatened since Reconstruction. Heflin was undoubtedly in sympathy with the reforms the Populists were seeking, but he wanted to bring them about from within the Democratic Party. He was elected to the Alabama legislature in 1896 over the strong opposition of the Populist candidate. He supported William Jennings Bryan for president that year after the "great Commoner" ran out on the Democratic-Populist fusion ticket of Bryan and Watson. Bryan had stuck with the Democratic nominee for vice president, Arthur Sewall.

With this kind of party loyalty throughout his political career from Mayor of Lafayette, Alabama, to United States Senator, it was not difficult to understand the uprising that took place in Alabama on December 16, 1929, as the state Democratic Committee, by a vote of 27-23, passed a resolution inviting anti-Smith Democrats back into the 1930 party primary but barring any opponent of the 1928 Democratic presidential nominee from running as a candidate.

Reaction was immediate. The committee vote itself indicated that there was plenty of opposition to such drastic action. Senator Hugo Black publicly opposed denying his colleagues the right to run in the primary, stating that such people "are never cowed by the cracking of party whips." Naturally there was disappointment, Black said, but rather than exact revenge the party should rebuild, looking ahead to the future, not back in anger at the past. Black, a former

Ku Klux Klan member, would have an important role in the upcoming senatorial contest.

Senator Heflin first set out to try to get the state committee to reverse its action. He made five speeches over the state designed to build up public support to get the committee to remove the bars which it had erected to keep him out of the primary. On New Year's Day, 1930, instead of listening to a football game, I found myself on a Southern Railway diner seventy miles from Birmingham eating hog jowls and black-eyed peas with Senator Heflin as we passed through the little town of Heflin, not directly connected to the senator's family.

Meanwhile, Senator Black had come out with an even stronger condemnation of the committee action, noting that "the law does not contemplate a special privileged class to run for office and a subordinate class who can vote but not hold office." In his opinion, the resolution might have been construed to bar from voting the thousands of Democrats who in 1928 had voted against Al Smith.

Heflin's chief legal advisor, Judge Horace Wilkinson, who had helped manage Bibb Graves's 1926 gubernatorial campaign and who was no novice to state politics, did not believe that the committee would reverse its actions and he started legal proceedings. A suit was filed and, by a split decision in *Wilkinson v. Henry*, the Alabama Supreme Court backed the committee. Having failed to get the committee to rescind its action and having exhausted all legal remedies, Senator Heflin had to face an important decision.

There was no question that, had he been permitted to enter the primary, he would have won renomination and re-election. His opponents realized this; hence, the December 16 resolution. Some of his followers urged him to enter the primary as a write-in candidate. There was no space on the ballot to write in the name of a candidate, and this was a risky business since he depended heavily upon support from rural voters of the state, many of whom would have difficulty casting a write-in vote. Others thought his name could be stamped in and Heflin seriously considered having 250,000 rubber stamps made up so that voters could vote for him without having to worry about the mechanics of writing in his name. At one point during the campaign, he showed me a few samples of the stamps. However, the state committee threatened not to recognize such ballots as legally cast.

With the party machinery solidly against him and no provision to conduct a write-in campaign, Heflin concluded he would have to abandon his effort to run in the primary. He decided to go along with his advisors, particularly Judge Wilkinson, who believed resentment against the committee was so strong Heflin could carry the state as an Independent in the November election, not only for himself, but for an anti-Smith Democratic candidate for governor as well. I thought Senator Heflin was taking on an extra burden in trying to do so; better he should run alone.

The "regular" Democratic primary was set for August 12, and John H. Bankhead, Jr., and Frederick I. Thompson were listed as the party candidates. Heflin traveled across the state urging his supporters to stay out of the election in order to "make this Raskob-Tammanyite primary look like a withered frog on a prairie."

Trouble was brewing, however. The party was beginning to tighten its screws. Representative George Huddleston, although a personal friend of the senator and politically sympathetic to his cause, wrote a fellow politician on July 20 that his "status as a beneficiary of the party organization required that [he] vote for the nominee in the primary" though he intended "to keep as far as possible out of any row between Heflin and his enemies."

Rumors abounded that the national Democratic party organization was getting set to intervene. I was traveling around the state with the Senator, eventually covering over one hundred of his speeches. At one stop I received information that Senator Pat Harrison and Governor Theodore Bilbo of Mississippi were planning to come to Alabama to lecture voters on party loyalty. On July 20, I wrote Vance that Hugo Black was fixing to fly the fence. Black would be up for reelection in 1932 and apparently he was receiving a lot of pressure from party leaders to remain loyal. Sure enough, after the primary he made over fifty speeches in behalf of the victorious Bankhead. This was not surprising, for in 1928 Black had taken a slow mail boat to Europe during the presidential campaign and left his political crowd in Alabama to wage the fight against Smith without his help.

The Heflin organization was immediately put on guard against what might happen in the general election by the way the election returns were handled. The newspapers at first announced that some 125,000 Alabamans had voted on August 12, 82,000 for Bankhead and 43,000 for Thompson. But there was a great deal of confusion. The results were supposed to be tabulated and announced by the secretary of state in Montgomery. A total vote of 125,000 was low, for there were 340,000 registered Democrats in Alabama. Heflin supporters were confident this indicated that two-thirds the state's Democratic voters had stayed out of the primary. Then it developed that Ed W. Pettus, chairman of the state committee, had taken the ballots to Selma where they were counted in the office of the tax assessor. Not until September 1st were the "official" primary victors announced. By this time Bankhead had 140,000 votes, Thomson 57,000, or a total of almost 200,000 Democratic votes—a more respectable party showing.

On the same day the "final totals" were announced, 3,500 Heflin Democrats gathered in convention in Montgomery to organize an independent party. Arthur Chilton, a Montgomery lawyer and an active anti-Smith Democrat, was chosen temporary chairman and J. B. Wadsworth, a Gadsden banker and an anti-Smith delegate at the Houston convention, was elected permanent chairman. Reverend J. T. Nelson, a ninety-eight-year-old Confederate veteran, made an address, during which he stated: "I have always been a Democrat. My father was a Democrat, and I married a Democratic woman. I never flew the track until Smith was nominated." Heflin was nominated for Senator, Judge Hugh Locke for Governor, and Dempsey M. Powell for Lieutenant Governor. They chose as their party emblem the liberty bell. Just how many Alabama Democrats would switch from the rooster, the symbol of the state party, to the liberty bell was hard to ascertain.

In 1930 the polling process in state elections had not been perfected, and about the only way observers could pick the potential winner was to compare the crowd each candidate drew on the stump. Radio was used on a limited basis during the 1930 campaign, but it did not suit the spread-eagle oratory of speakers like Heflin. In many ways he patterned his stump speeches after William Jennings Bryan, but with one added ingredient. That was Heflin's ability to tell stories which not only amused his audiences but often illustrated the political point he was trying to drive home. This and his identification with his rural constituents greatly added to his following.

During the quarter century Heflin was in Congress he became nationally recognized as the best storyteller on Capitol Hill, so much so that many congressmen at the opposite end of the political spectrum from Heflin seldom missed an opportunity to hear the Alabaman speak, either on the House and Senate floors or in the cloakrooms. He appeared to have an inexhaustible repertoire of anecdotes.

Senator Royal S. Copeland of New York said: "There can be no doubt that Senator Heflin is one of the most remarkable storytellers in the United States." He noted that Senator Henry Cabot Lodge used to follow him around to hear his stories and, as for himself, he remarked, "I have laughed over them until I have nearly split my sides." He received similar accolades from scores of his other colleagues, many of whom were gifted storytellers themselves.

Visitors to the Senate galleries marveled at this massive, black-frocked figure who discoursed, often without notes, for hours on a subject of deep concern to him. Interspersed were anecdotes, innuendos and little turns of speech designed to render his opponents helpless and to prove his point. Arthur Krock, of the *New York Times*, once criticized Heflin as "loud, narrow and vindictive," but he had to admit that the Alabaman had "a certain outrageous and winning bravado" and "as a ranconteur was exceptionally gifted."

In covering his speeches in Alabama in 1930, I never grew tired of hearing him or of watching the reactions of his audiences, day after day. Despite hearing the same stories at each stop, it was still sheer amusement to me. Wherever he spoke, the courthouse, the fairground or the auditorium would be overflowing. He had a tremendous voice and could speak for hours without the aid of loudspeakers and still retain a vocal magnitude which could reach those ears at the farthest edges of his audience.

By contrast, his opponent, John Bankhead could barely muster a crowd, despite the efforts of the Democratic leaders to make it appear he was the people's choice. Later Heflin would enjoy telling of a speech Bankhead made over radio from a courtroom with 480 seats in it. By air time only a handful of people had shown up. Bankhead began by telling everyone how grateful he was "for this great outpouring of the people." Apparently some latecomers then arrived. Jerome Fuller, an Alabama power company official, jumped up and shouted, "Don't leave gentlemen, there are plenty of vacant seats in the rear."

I went to several of Bankhead's speeches and they were sparsely attended, dry affairs in comparison with the Heflin meetings. John Bankhead was no doubt effective in arguing a case in court but he was not cut out for speaking on the political hustings. On the other hand, his brother Congressman Will Bankhead, father of Tallulah, was an effective speaker on the stump.

As the campaign progressed, the fur began to fly. Heflin charged that the committee's action had been dictated by outside interests (Smith forces) who wanted to dominate Alabama politics. If he was to be punished for his role in the defeat of Smith in 1928, then the place to do it was in the primary. He pointed out that all Democrats were being taxed to pay for the primary, yet some of them were deprived of their rights by not being allowed to run or to vote for all the candidates of their choice.

In defending his action in not supporting Al Smith for president, Heflin, whose favorite sport was fox hunting, enjoyed telling his rural audiences about how the country dog put one over on the city dog.

> You know I used to have an old strike dog, old Jack, and whenever old Jack barked it was a fox. The other dogs would bark and tear up and down the swamp and the old fox hunters wouldn't say anything. Some of the boys would say, "I have got one up." They would say, "No, I haven't heard old Jack and Lee and Claude." And when you would hear them, then they would throw their legs over the saddle and pull up the reins and say, "Let's go, boys, it's a fox." I am an old strike dog of the Democratic party and when you put the candidate out in front of me he must be a Democratic fox or I won't run him.

This would bring applause and he would follow up with:

> A country dog went into town and asked a town dog what he ran for sport. He said house cats. "Why," he said, "you ain't got any sport at all." The town dog said, "What do you run?" He said, "Rabbits, squirrels, possums, coons, and foxes." "Oh," the town dog said, "it is great sport running cats," and looking down toward the swamp below the house he saw a beautiful little black and white striped cat out of the range of smell, and he said, "Yonder goes one now." The country dog said, "We don't run that kind." The town dog said, "I am going to catch him and kill him," and he dashed off after this cat. He came back in a little while. He was scratching his nose in the grass and he was chewing every kind of grass he could get hold of, and he was rolling and groaning in the weeds and this country dog said, "Did you kill him?" and he said, "No, by golly, he gassed me."

As the laughter died down, Heflin would shout: "Al Smith and his Tammany crowd gassed me. No, I did not support him and I have no apology to make for doing what I believed was best for my party and my country." This would bring forth another round of applause.

Heflin never let down on the twenty-seven state Democratic Committee members who voted to deny him the right to run for reelection in the primary.

He said they had their own axes to grind and would tell a story about meat stealing:

> A person was caught stealing a rump of meat [he said]. He went into trial showing no concern as the lawyers prosecuted him before the jury. As the evidence was presented showing that he had clearly stolen the meat, his attorney noticed that his client was absolutely unconcerned and he turned to him and said, "Don't you worry about the case they are making against you?" "Not at all," he replied. His attorney asked why, and he answered, "Because all twelve of the jurors got some of the meat."

"All twenty-seven got some of the meat," Heflin would say.

But he turned back to the Bible in assailing the "twenty-seven" for creating the two classes of Democrats—one who could vote in the primary and another who could vote but not run for public office.

> You know back in the old biblical days, old Nahash began to move with his army against Jabesh. And Jabesh saw that there was a pretty good number of them, and he went to Nahash and said, "If you will make a covenant with us we will serve you." Old Nahash said, "I will covenant with you if you will let me pluck out your right eyes!"
>
> They were going to have to lose their right eyes to go in so that they would be helpless for defensive purposes. And this bunch, they want to pluck out the right eye of your leader, your Democratic senator, put his right eye out, deprive him of the right to run, but they want you to vote for somebody they put up. Half slave and half free! They can't put that over in Alabama. We will repudiate it. Alabama will repudiate it.

Heflin noted Bankhead had held only one elected office, as road commissioner of Walker County. Heflin charged his opponent was "a subservient agent of the million-dollar corporations," having been on the payroll of the Southern Railroad, the Mobile and Ohio Railroad, the Alabama Power Company and several large mining companies. He had had to resign from the board of trustees of the University of Alabama because the board voiced its approval of a plan to tax the coal mines in support of higher education. Then-governor Thomas E. Kilby had denounced Bankhead's resignation, stating: "Any man who would desert the boys and girls of Alabama in favor of coal mine owners was not fit to serve on the board of any educational institution."

Reporting in those days was quite different from what it is today. Newspapers took strong and active positions in support of or against political candidates. Reporters followed the positions of their editors and their news stories were written to carry out the objectives of the newspaper for which they worked. It was in this role, more or less, that I covered the Heflin campaign and my advocacy of Heflin was no different from that of the reporters of the big Montgomery, Birmingham and Mobile daily papers in their support of Bankhead.

While in Jasper, I also dug up information that John Bankhead had on one occasion struck three white men from a jury list in order to include a black, something sure to be resented by the white-supremacy-minded voters in northern Alabama. I found one of of the jury members, Rufus M. Tidwell, who gladly signed a notarized affidavit to that effect. That was political dynamite in those days in Alabama.

Heflin also charged Bankhead had concocted some sort of fake patented medicine and sold it to farmers around the state, claiming his "pellagra juice" would cure the disease. Medical science at that time knew virtually nothing about treating pellagra and Heflin would often refer to his opponent as "Pellagra John."

Another charge by the Bankhead faction dealt with Heflin's stand on prohibition. They claimed that Heflin was anti-prohibition because he had voted against the submission of the Eighteenth Amendment to the states. Bankhead forces charged that the fact that his son, J. Thomas Heflin, Jr., had been arrested several times for public drunkenness proved Heflin was misleading the people. The press had somehow gotten word that young Heflin had apparently become intoxicated on a boat trip to Panama in March of 1929. One month later he faced the possibility of a lawsuit for attacking a Greenwich Village taxi driver. In June he was arrested in Washington on the charge of operating an automobile while under the influence of a narcotic. And in September he failed to appear in court to answer another charge of intoxication and of violating the Alabama prohibition law.

Heflin's son caused his father tremendous worry but the senator stood by him. He tried to rebut the charge by stating that the Panama incident was a case where the senator's enemies had "encouraged the young man to take a drink as a cure for seasickness." After the 1930 campaign, young Heflin reformed, married, and began to lead a normal life. Then, tragically, in 1934 he was killed in an automobile accident.

As for Prohibition, Heflin had supported an amendment to the state constitution in 1909 and at the time thought the state method was the best way. When the constitutional amendment was passed, he became an ardent supporter.

During the campaign, Heflin stressed his long record of service to the people of Alabama. He had helped lead the fight for direct election of senators. He had led the crackdown on W.P.G. "Poison Gas" Harding and driven him from the Federal Reserve Board after his politics led to the "deflation panic" of 1920. He had secured passage of legislation designed to enable the Federal Trade Commission to break up the cotton seed trust. He had helped to pass the farm loan banking system law. He fought unrestricted immigration and had been a leading spokesman for the national public education bill. And last, but certainly not least, Heflin was the author of a joint resolution establishing Mother's Day.

Despite the large crowds he was drawing and his effective oratory, I sensed that Heflin was in trouble. I wrote Vance to explain the situation. The Senator had powerful opposition which was organized to the hilt. Meanwhile J. L. Thornton, Heflin's secretary, caring little whether he cooperated with anyone, sat in his office in Lafayette thinking his boss would win the fight by mailing out his campaign speeches. James Esdale and Earl Hotalen of the Klan were working to promote *The Menace*, an anti-Catholic publication, and were hardly speaking to Judge Locke, Judge Wilkinson and the others. Worse, the owner of the only Alabama paper on He-flin's side, H. H. Golson of the *Abbeville Independent,* was hesitant to wed himself to the liberty bell. He insisted on making his paper the official publication even though it only had a circulation of 10,000 and had no facilities or personnel to increase that figure. The *Forum* was strong for Heflin but could only devote so much space to the Alabama campaign, although some special Alabama editions were printed.

Meanwhile, *The Birmingham News and Age Herald* and the *Montgomery Advertiser,* called by Heflin the "Montgomery Fertilizer," were strong for Bankhead. The only articles in these papers about Heflin were ones attacking the veteran Senator. This was ironic because Frank Glass of the *Advertiser* had been a leader of the Democrats who bolted Bryan in 1896 to support "Sound Money" Democrat John M. Palmer, ad-vising his readers, "Follow Your Convictions."

Heflin also had to contend with increasing hard times, as the specter of deep economic depression began to cast its shadow across Alabama. I wrote Vance that, in my opinion, hard times and eleven-cent cotton were beginning to hurt Heflin more than anything else. There was a jingle going around the state:

> Hoover blew the whistle,
> DePriest rang the bell,
> Heflin yelled, "All-a-board,"
> And business went to hell.

Others asked, "Do you belong to the 4-H Club? Hoover, He-flin, Hell and Hard Times?"

I told Vance the Heflin people in Alabama were the bro-kest crowd I had ever seen. I knew for a fact Senator Heflin was having to obtain loans to carry on his campaign since he received too little financial help from his friends. However, Vance was skeptical of my plea of hard times, especially as it affected increasing the circulation of the *Forum* in Alabama. He wrote back: "I don't believe a lack of money is the whole trouble. If you will check the picture shows and gasoline sta-tions, you will see they have plenty of money for those."

In the middle of all this, the Senator and I almost lost our lives in a car wreck. The morning after a Heflin speech in Decatur, we got back into his Buick touring car and headed for Anniston and then on to Montgomery. Heflin and his son were in the back seat and I was in the front with Heflin's nephew Perry Schuessler. I was reading the Tennessee primary results where Senator William Brock was elected to the short term. Heflin wanted to know how Cordell Hull had done in the long-term race. I was scanning the pages looking for the results when I heard someone yell, "Watch that truck!" I looked up to see our car heading toward a truck loaded with logs, which had pulled across the road. Schuessler wisely decided to swing out of the road and up against a telephone pole. Had he not done so we would all have been decapitated by the heavy logs. There was a crashing of glass and a snapping of metal; then everything went blank.

When I came to, I was on the ground by the car with my feet up against the side of the car. Heflin was on top of me with his foot caught under the front seat. I could see nothing, and I thought I had lost my eyesight. I began wiping the blood from my eyes and it was a great feeling when I realized I could see again. Heflin managed to get his foot released and then walked over to a bench at a nearby filling station. Within ten minutes we were all on our feet, with only the Senator's son and me bleeding badly.

A bus came by and carried us back to Decatur, where everyone except Heflin checked into the hospital. He got a room at the hotel and called a friend to drive him on to Anniston. After a two-hour speech, Senator Heflin was examined and found to have a sprained back, cuts on his leg, and a sprained arm. Still, after a few hour's rest, he got up again and was driven to Montgomery.

Young Heflin was badly cut and had a sprained back. Schuessler was cut over the eye and had a broken rib. I had a mean cut close to my right eye and my nose was broken in two places. A doctor at the local hospital set my nose and, after spending the night, I left for Montgomery by train. After throwing my things in the Pullman, I went into the diner to eat. I must have been a sorry sight. The fellow across from me finally got up and moved to another seat in the diner rather than have his dinner looking at the cuts and bruises all over my face.

After covering Heflin's Montgomery meeting, I joined my wife in Atlanta. While there I consulted a specialist who recommended an operation to break and reset my nose. Later I checked with Senator Heflin's brother, a doctor in Birmingham. He was a good doctor and a fine gentleman and he told me that the doctors in Decatur had done a pretty good job and it would be foolish to have my nose broken again and reset. I followed his advice.

Despite the problems the Heflin campaign was having, Heflin and many of his supporters concluded that, based on the tremendous crowds he was drawing in every section of the state, he would win re-election to the Senate by an overwhelming majority.

I was in Birmingham election night, and before one-fourth of the votes were counted, it was obvious the popular support generated by Heflin during the campaign had not carried over to the ballot box. The Democratic machine had done its work. Supporters at Heflin headquarters were flabbergasted. Judge Wilkinson was convinced political chicanery at the ballot box had prevented the liberty bell from ringing out a victory over the Democratic rooster.

I was supposed to send in hourly reports to the Vance operated radio station, WJSV, in Washington but I conceded the election to Bankhead early in the evening. Then I adjourned to a bar to commiserate with Heflin's friends. The final totals gave Bankhead 150,985 votes and Heflin 100,969.

The Heflin opponents in Alabama were jubilant over the general election results and, needless to say, Senator Heflin was stunned as he saw the seat he had held in the Senate for ten years slipping away from him. He immediately charged John Bankhead's election was rigged and announced plans to contest his right to sit in the Senate.

With Judge Wilkinson as his chief legal consultant, Heflin laid plans to convince the United States Senate to have

Senator-elect Bankhead stand aside when he appeared to take the oath in the new Congress when it convened. Heflin's term did not end until March 1931 and he had until the end of the lame duck session to build up support for an investigation into the Alabama election. He relied on two arguments for denying Bankhead his seat: that the Democratic primary election in which Bankhead had been nominated was illegal and morally wrong and that the November general election itself was corrupt.

The Democratic leadership in the Senate, led by Joe Robinson who had been Al Smith's running mate in 1928 and whom Heflin had challenged vigorously in the 1928 campaign, swung into action, determined to seat Bankhead. This was in sharp contrast to the Democratic support given the successful effort in 1927 to deny Republican William Vare from Pennsylvania a Senate seat in a similar contest.

But when March 4, 1931, rolled around, John Bankhead was not asked to stand aside and was permitted to take the oath and be seated without prejudice. Senator Heflin had to vacate his spacious offices but the Republican-controlled Senate gave him a temporary office on the ground floor while his contest was pending. During this period he conducted himself as though he were still the senior Senator from Alabama to the great discomfort of Hugo Black who now claimed that title. His intense activity to keep his seat also frayed the nerves of some of his former colleagues, who increasingly desired to bring the whole affair to a close.

Still, the matter dragged on. The case was being handled by the Committee on Privileges and Elections, chaired by Samuel Morgan Shortridge of California, on which there was a nine-to-eight Republican majority.

After the committee voted 9-8 on April 16, 1932 to recommend the contest be dropped, Heflin, in an extremely close vote, was given the right to address the Senate. The day of Heflin's speech, the Senate galleries were packed and the corridors were lined with people wanting to get in to hear what everyone knew would be a dramatic appearance by one of the Senate's most gifted orators. Eighty-seven senators an-

swered the roll. The press gallery was packed with what Heflin liked to call the "hickory-nut-headed" reporters of
Washington. Most of them pictured Heflin at one time or another as a man who had lost his equilibrium in becoming so
fanatical about the Pope and the Catholic church. Still, they
recognized Heflin's speaking ability and did not want to miss
this historic and histrionic show.

For five hours and twelve minutes Tom Heflin occupied
the floor, the two-hour limit having been dispensed with at
the request of Senator Norris, with the unanimous consent of
the Senate. Quoting the Bible, Bryon, the U.S. Constitution
and a host of contemporary political writers, he presented
what he considered to be a damning case against the Alabama state executive committee and their candidate. He criticized the Machiavellian machinations of committee chairman
Ed Pettus. Heflin castigated Senator Hugo Black for his two-
faced role in the process. He complained that he had lined up
hours and hours of more testimony which would have shown
convincingly the "stealing and skullduggery" that occurred.
Point by point, he examined the irregularities at the polling
places, the improperly handled ballots, the stacks of marked
ballots found still attached to their original pads, the intimi-
dation and challenging of Heflin voters, the deliberate un-
der-representation of Heflin officials at the polling sites, the
illegal solicitations of absentee ballots, the purchasing of
votes, the illegal and premature opening of ballot boxes, the
burning of some boxes, the voting of absentee voters without
their knowledge and the forged primary vote. Stories, twists
of speech and tales of chivalry and honor were interwoven
with this list of high crimes by Bankhead and the state committee against the people of Alabama.

In referring to the action of his colleague, Black, whom
Heflin had supported for the Senate in 1926 when he was an
unknown police court judge in Birmingham, Senator Heflin
pulled out a tear-jerker from his repertoire of stories. As he
described his feeling, he said:

> There was a widower in the rural area who was left with a
> young son to raise. The farmer subsequently met a widow, who

also had a young son, and they were married. Soon they drove out to town in their wagon to do some shopping. The farmer bought for his stepson some nice patent leather shoes and for his own son he only bought some rough working shoes. As they drove home, the farmer looked in the back of his wagon and saw his son crying. "What is the matter, son, do your new shoes hurt your feet?" "No," the son replied. "I hurt here," and put his hand on his heart.

But the die was cast and the Senate was not to be moved by oratory.

On April 28, the Senate took up final consideration of the Alabama contest. The vote then proceeded on the resolution to declare the seat vacant. Nineteen Republicans voted "yea," thirty-eight Democrats, twenty-four Republicans, and one Independent voted "nay." Then the Senate, by a vote of 64 to 18, gave the seat to Bankhead.

Heflin reacted:

> It is a travesty on justice. . . . It marks a sad decline in Democratic leadership and control. It is a triumph for crooked and corrupt practices employed in behalf of a Democrat. . . . I have just begun to fight. I am particularly hurt at the unfair and unkind treatment accorded me by Senator Black.

The year 1932 found Heflin back in the Democratic camp vigorously supporting the nomination and election of Franklin D. Roosevelt. Heflin had charged in the 1930 campaign that Smith would again be a candidate for president in 1932. His prediction came true as Smith, along with Raskob, was in Chicago doing his best to keep the man who had dubbed him the "Happy Warrior" from receiving the two-thirds necessary for nomination. This, of course, resulted in the Garner-for-vice-president deal which released the Texas delegation's votes and assured Roosevelt's nomination.

In 1934, Heflin ran for Congress but was defeated. Afterward, I gradually lost touch with the senator, although we corresponded for a time on an irregular basis. With Roosevelt as president, Heflin received a federal job in Alabama. One day in late 1937, when the ex-senator had come to Washington for an appointment at one of the federal agencies, he came out to my house for dinner. We discussed politics and particularly what President Roosevelt had done under the New Deal for the people suffering from the depression. Sitting around after our meal, he looked at me and in all seriousness said, "You know, Walter, I am at peace with the world—including the Pope." This was an interesting statement by a man who after almost four decades of political service to his party and his state had lost his Senate seat due to the action of twenty-seven members of a state committee.

When Hugo Black was appointed to the U.S. Supreme Court in 1937, Heflin announced for his vacant seat, running against the progressive Lister Hill. His opening speech contained the same old "Heflinisms" and some new ones: emphasis on protecting the cotton farmer, attacking the increasing power of the labor movement and attacking Roosevelt's court-packing plan. But by then his time had passed. He had sent me a copy of his speech and asked for comments. I was sorry to have to contradict some of the Senator's statements, particularly those claiming there were no sweatshops or child labor problems in Alabama. Although Heflin referred to Roosevelt as "the greatest man who ever lived," he followed the line espoused by Jimmy Byrnes in the Senate against the Wage and Hour Law Bill. Nothing would have given Heflin more pleasure than being elected to the seat vacated by Hugo Black. However, he went down to defeat by a 2 to 1 vote. He was stricken by pneumonia and almost died on election day and was not told of his defeat until a week later.

In 1895, Heflin had married Minnie Kayle Schuessler, whose family had some money, and they built a beautiful Southern colonial-type home in Lafayette with large Greek relief columns, a typical residence for a member of Congress. His wife, however, did not like Washington society and remained in Alabama but some of Heflin's letters to her while he was in Congress—now in the Heflin collection at the University of Alabama in Tuscaloosa—showed his continued deep love for his wife, who died while their son Tom was just a child. In his last years, the old Senator had to rent out the downstairs of his home to make ends meet. Then there was no government pension for retired or defeated members of Congress. The Senator became senile and, after his death, when people were going through his papers, they found checks from the government which he had failed to cash.

On July 30, 1935, Heflin was granted a patent for an instrument for use in massaging the hair and scalp. He had hopes of selling this and using his own fine head of hair as an advertising gimmick. However, nothing ever came of it.

Heflin's last picture, taken in his upstairs room at his home in Lafayette, shows him with one hand resting on a cane, wearing the same bow tie, his nose-pinching glasses and ribbon and his old and wrinkled white suit. No longer was he immaculately dressed, and time had taken its toll on his robust body. At 4:30 p.m. on April 26, 1951, he died. Clare Purcell, Methodist Bishop of Alabama, delivered the funeral oration. He quoted from the tombstone of James L. Petigru in St. Michael's churchyard in Charleston. This quotation, under the seal of the Senate, is on Heflin's tombstone in Lafayette:

> Unawed by opinion,
> Unseduced by flattery
> Undismayed by disaster
> He confronted life with antique courage
> And death with Christian hope

What Senator George F. Hoar of Massachusetts said of Senator John T. Morgan, who served Alabama in the Senate for thirty years, could also be said of Tom Heflin: "He came here a poor man. He went out a poor man."

My involvement in the Heflin senatorial bid was a small but an important chapter of my life. I wouldn't have missed it for the world. The 1930 Alabama campaign was an exciting reporting experience for me and, based on what I observed and learned there, it enabled me to be of much assistance years later when I helped manage Strom Thurmond's successful write-in campaign for the United States Senate. I must admit that it was advocacy journalism to the nth degree as my participation reflects. But I was convinced a wrong had been done which needed correcting at the ballot box. Little did I realize that twenty-four years later another state Democratic committee would undertake to name a U.S. Senator for a six-year term by avoiding a primary and I would become involved.

Epilogue

My commitment to the Watson legacy grew over the years. My fond remembrances of Hickory Hill endeared the place to me, and I kept an ever-watchful eye over the estate during the post-Watson years. After Mr. and Mrs. Watson died, the estate was divided between his two granddaughters after a number of bequests had been settled for other members of his family. In addition to his property in and near Thomson, consisting of several houses and over 250 acres adjoining Hickory Hill, he owned several thousand acres of farm land.

Watson's will was broken and under the subsequent settlement, Hickory Hill and most of the adjoining property was left to Georgia Watson and the old Watson home and about 60 acres of adjoining land was left to my future wife, Georgia Lee, whom I married April 12, 1925. Jessie Watson and Oscar Lee, the surviving parents of Watson's granddaughters, were appointed administrators of the estate and undertook to divide it equally between their children.

My wife had died in 1935 from a lung sarcoma and tuberculosis. In 1938, Georgia Watson married Dr. Avery O. Craven, professor of Southern history at the University of Chicago. Following the death of Mrs. Watson, Hickory Hill

Thousands Pay Tribute to Tom Watson As Statue Is Unveiled on Capitol Lawn

Left to right: Miss Georgia Watson (granddaughter of Senator Watson) and Miss Eleanor Watson (a grandniece) at the dedication of the Watson monument on the capitol grounds in Atlanta.

deteriorated and at one time it was placed on the market. The Rural Free Delivery mail carriers almost bought it to establish a memorial to the author of the RFD legislation.

After their marriage, the Cravens decided to move to Hickory Hill. They remodeled the residence, eliminating some of the structure—including the back part of the house, which contained the dining room, aviary, living room and kitchen—but preserving the main body. The back living room was converted into the kitchen and an adjoining bathroom became a breakfast room which connected with one of the larger rooms that became the dining room. They installed modern plumbing, central heating and made it more livable. However, they soon found that Dr. Craven—in his work as a historian—needed to be nearer Chicago; and Mrs. Craven offered to sell me her half of the Watson estate, including Hickory Hill, which I purchased in 1947. As guardian for my minor son, Tom Watson Brown, I looked after his half of the estate as well. During the intervening years, I spent much time and money putting the Watson estate back together and preserving and improving Hickory Hill, which is now on the Historic Register, and the surrounding grounds. In addition to acquiring much of the original furniture, I preserved and restored the various outbuildings; and Hickory Hill, with the exception of the back structure eliminated by Mrs. Craven, is much like it was when Watson lived. The *Jeffersonian* printing plant building was sold by Jessie Watson and torn down in the 1920s. I deeded this site to the Watson-Brown Foundation which I have established primarily to aid young boys and girls in need of a college education. The Foundation has moved to the *Jeffersonian* publishing plant site and restored the log cabin in which Watson was born in 1856 on the old Watson homestead some five miles out of Thomson.

My father lived a full life after his defeat as Commissioner of Agriculture in 1926. Because of his political connec-

"Hickory Hill"—Thomas E. Watson's home in Thomson, Georgia.

tions, papa became an agronomist involved in developing the Okefenokee Swamp near Waycross as a state park. He was given a position with the Georgia Wildlife Commission. He helped handle the transfer of deer and other wildlife to the Clarks Hill Reservoir near Thomson, which made that area a hunter's paradise.

But after 1927, my father was never again to hold an elective political office. He was badly defeated when he subsequently ran against Gene Talmadge for Commissioner in 1930. He also ran for Congress in his South Georgia home district in 1940 and was defeated.

But on that day in 1927 when papa left for forced retirement to his heavily mortgaged Appling County farm near the county seat, Baxley, he was a sad man. I have never felt as sorry for anyone as I did for him then. He had previously sold our home in Bowman, over my mother's objection, to invest in South Georgia farmland. This meant my parents had no

J. J. Brown runs for Congress in 1940 and is defeated.

home to return to except a six-room farmhouse, which was adequate, but was certainly a let-down from our rambling home in Bowman or the rented Victorian place on Capitol Square in Atlanta.

But papa and mama tackled their new task in making a living off the farm with the same zeal and determination they had when they were first married, again working side by side in the field. My mother always planted a little cotton patch when they lived on the farm, but her pride and joy was her butter. When the Hoover depression came along, it was her "butter money" that enabled them to procure staples like coffee, sugar, salt and spices from Ray's Grocery in Baxley and always to have good and wholesome meals.

As a young girl living near Little Holly Springs after the Civil War, my mother had seen her relatives so poor they had to bury a loved one wrapped only in a sheet. She lived in fear of not being properly buried and she always had tucked away in her trunk enough butter money to buy a coffin. She never agreed with papa's politics, but when defeat came, she was ready to start life over again in a modest farmhouse with no modern conveniences. She was a loyal wife and a wonderful mother who never ceased telling her children they would never amount to anything without an education. She taught me the value of a dollar and gave me one lesson in life I have always followed: Be happy in your work or get out!

The farm was a fine body of land of nearly a thousand acres. Much of it was in virgin pine timber and could have tided my parents over their financial difficulties. However, my brother-in-law, Carl Teasley, ran into financial difficulty at the Bank of Toccoa largely as a result of speculation activities, including building a railroad from Toccoa to Carnesville. Papa had to sell off this timber to get him out of trouble. In the end, he sold the Appling County farm and bought a smaller farm on U.S. 1., three miles from Alma in Bacon County, which adjoined Appling. This home was much more desirable than the isolated Burke place near Baxley. He had been able to acquire his farm near Alma by assuming a federal land bank loan. He got behind in his payments during

Brown family photographed on their farm near Alma, Georgia on U. S. Highway No. 1.

the depression, but under the policies of the Franklin Roosevelt administration, he was able to refinance the loan and hold onto this farm. Subsequently, however, I concluded it would be best for him and my mother to move to the old Tom Watson home in Thomson to operate the Watson farms which my son had inherited. Convinced by the arguments that they needed to be closer to other people and to have modern home conveniences because of their age, they agreed.

In 1934 papa was stabbed by an itinerant farm worker he had employed temporarily. The man was out of a job and papa let him live in one of the houses on the new farm. They got into an argument. Papa, then 69, was fully capable of taking care of himself in any kind of physical encounter. But before he realized it, the man came at him with a knife and stabbed him in the chest. Papa was in great pain and he was

Mrs. Captora Ginn Brown, wife of J. J. Brown. Photographed while living at the old Tom Watson home, Thomson, Georgia.

taken to the hospital in Waycross. Fortunately, the blade struck his breastbone and failed to puncture his lung. Papa soon recovered and enjoyed good health for the rest of his life.

Papa was an ardent supporter of Roosevelt because he saw in the New Deal the realization of some of the things he had been advocating since the days he began following Watson and the Populist movement. However, he did have some misgivings. During my stay in Georgia in 1933, I accompanied him to a field of cotton in full bloom where Dock Smith, a black Watson tenant farmer, had to plow up a large part of his crop to comply with the Agricultural Adjustment Act. As we watched him guide his mule, which was pulling a middle buster and uprooting the rows of cotton, one by one, my father turned to me and said: "Walter, there is something wrong with our system when Dock Smith has to plow up that fine field of cotton and he is so poor he is wearing a jute guano sack for a shirt." Papa later felt the same way about killing little pigs when so many people in the country and in the world were hungry.

Papa died in 1953, and my mother followed three years later. My father reached the age of eighty-eight less ten days, and my mother lived two days after celebrating her ninetieth birthday. Papa's funeral at the Holly Springs Baptist Church just across Beaverdam Creek from Bowman was one of the last of the old-time political funerals and one he would have enjoyed. Political leaders from Georgia and South Carolina attended, including such political celebrities as James F. Byrnes, whom my father idolized, and Strom Thurmond whom Papa supported for President in 1948. Our family preacher, Seaborn Winn, was an outstanding politician in his own right and he could not resist the temptation to glorify Tom Watson, J. J. Brown and their causes, delivering a eulogy which lasted nearly an hour. As the grandsons of J.J. Brown rolled the casket out of the church, I leaned over to touch it and to say good-bye to my father, remembering the words of my good friend Judge Cecil Wyche who told me life is never the same for a man after his father is gone. On the slab over the grave, I put these words from 2 Timothy:

> I have fought a good fight. I have finished my course. I have kept the faith.